While the Pasta Cooks

While the Pasta Cooks

100 Sauces So Easy You Can Prepare the Sauce
in the Time It Takes to Cook the Pasta

By Andrew Schloss with Ken Bookman

Macmillan • USA

MACMILLAN
A Simon & Schuster Macmillan Company
1633 Broadway
New York, NY 10019

Library of Congress Cataloging-in-Publication Data
Schloss, Andrew, 1951–
    While the pasta cooks: 100 sauces so easy you can prepare the sauce in the time it takes to cook the pasta/by Andrew Schloss with Ken Bookman.
         p.   cm.
   Includes index.
   ISBN: 0-02-860989-1
    1. Cookery (Pasta) 2. Sauces.   I. Title.
TX809.M17S25   1996
641.8'22—dc20   95-44743
                                                      CIP

Manufactured in the United States of America

10 9 8 7 6 5 4 3 2 1

Book design by Rachael McBrearty

Dedication

To Karen, with love—and a little sauce.

A.S.

To my parents, Thelma and Jack Bookman, with love, gratitude, and a reminder that I was never a picky eater when we had spaghetti for dinner.

K.B.

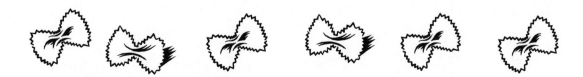

Contents

Acknowledgments

When authors have worked on four cookbooks together, as is our case, there's a natural tendency to look at the many people who've helped to see who has been there from the start. Among publishing people, we have one name, Judith Weber, our literary agent. She must like our book ideas before anyone else gets the chance to dislike them, and we couldn't ask for a better critic.

We had never before worked with Justin Schwartz, our editor at Macmillan, but he has been a friend of this book from the start. We thank him for that and for the fine editing he did with both his pencil and his taste buds. Our copyeditor, Virginia Croft, with good judgment and a good eye, helped our manuscript nicely, and Rachael McBrearty, a most talented designer, applied her considerable talent to creating a beautiful package for this book. Our thanks to them too.

They aren't publishing people, but they've been with us from the start, too: the other people who live in our respective homes. A book project hovers over a home for months, and we thank the tolerant and supportive people who dealt with that so graciously—Karen Shain Schloss; Dana, Issac, and Ben Schloss; and Ruth Adelman.

Andrew Schloss and Ken Bookman

Preface

It's got to be because pasta is so much fun. There can't be any other explanation. There are plenty of cheap foods. There are plenty of nutritious foods. There are plenty of versatile, tasty, quick, and easy foods. But there's only one food that's accurately described by *all* those words: pasta.

So prepare to have some fun with your cooking and to fall in love with what you'll create.

And while you're at it, remember that there's a strong practical side to a pasta dinner. I think the most striking thing about the recipes you're about to read is how many of them need no more accompaniment than a simple salad and a wedge of bread to make a complete meal. And dozens of these pasta sauces go even further, producing a full one-dish meal—starch, meat, and vegetable all on one plate.

Over the years, food after food has burst upon the culinary scene with a mad rush of recipes—and then just as quickly vanished. So you may wonder why you should add this cookbook to your pasta repertoire.

Like our first three cookbooks, this one is driven by *our* concern for *your* time. And if we can debunk a myth or two along the way, better still. The image you probably hold of the long-simmered pasta sauce, lovingly coaxed along over the afternoon hours, just doesn't fit with today's lifestyle. Every sauce in this book will be ready for the pasta even before the pasta is ready for the sauce. If we couldn't make a sauce in the time it took to boil the water and cook the pasta, then we won't ask you to make it either.

True to the title of the book, each of these sauces can be prepared by a typical home cook in no more time than it takes to bring a few quarts of water to a boil and cook the pasta. When we started out, our time frame assumed that you'd be using dried pasta, which cooks in 10 minutes or so, not fresh pasta, which cooks in just 2 or 3. But soon we realized that most of these sauces could be prepared even in that shorter time, after you've brought the pasta water to a boil.

I use the word "we" loosely when I speak of the recipes because their creation is the work of my collaborator, Andrew Schloss. You're in good hands when you cook from his recipes. I often refer to him as a human recipe machine. Of the dozens of food professionals I've worked with over the years, I've never known anyone with as extensive a mental catalog of taste and flavor combinations. His cooking imagination constantly pushes him to try out new combinations, and his good taste buds tell him when he has gone too far.

Andrew and I have worked together for more than 13 years, beginning when I was the food editor of *The Philadelphia Inquirer* and I hired him as a regular contributor. Our collaboration on newspaper food articles led seamlessly to our collaboration producing cookbooks. This is our fourth book, and although all four cover different topics with different approaches, they share a fundamental belief: that good cooking and time-crunched lifestyles can coexist—with a little help.

Our first book, *Fifty Ways to Cook Most Everything: 2500 Creative Solutions to the Daily Dilemma of What to Cook*, sought to get home cooks out of their recipe ruts with hundreds of tiny but impressive recipes that would bring variety into the home kitchen. We followed that with *Dinner's Ready: Turn a Single Meal Into a Week of Dinners*, which brought restaurant tricks into the home kitchen to show how home cooks could set out preparing five dinners with hardly more effort than it took to prepare one. And our third book, *One-Pot Cakes: 60 Recipes for Cakes from Scratch Using a Pot, a Spoon, and a Pan*, streamlined the typical cake into a 10-minute preparation virtually free of bowls and long cleanups.

We hope this book, too, will put some good food on your table—food that might not otherwise have gotten there.

Ken Bookman

Introduction

Using This Book

Preparing a pasta meal is about as simple as cooking can get. This book is intended to keep that simplicity while expanding your repertoire of sauces well beyond what you might have thought possible without going out and buying something prepared.

As with any activity, no matter how simple, a brief tour will help you do a better and quicker job. Here, then, is a primer on pasta cooking, sauce ingredients, and relevant techniques.

Ingredients

Pasta

There are two styles of pasta. Flat-profile noodles, such as fettuccine, lasagna, and ravioli, are made with eggs and can be either fresh or dried. Round-profile noodles, such as spaghetti, macaroni, and wagon wheels, are made without egg and are always dried.

Trying to make a quality distinction between dried pasta and fresh is meaningless. Either style can achieve beautifully textured, *al dente* perfection, just as either style can produce dismal results. A lot depends on the quality of the

individual product. The best advice I can give you is to try different brands until you find one you like—and different cooking times until you find the pasta texture you prefer. Then stick with both the brand and the cooking time. I aim for a pasta texture that offers slight resistance to the teeth (that's the meaning of the Italian phrase *al dente*) and with no remaining raw taste. As for brand, at this writing I cannot recommend any nationally distributed brand. Throughout the country, however, you will find several high-quality regionally distributed brands.

But choosing the right pasta for a particular sauce is another matter. To some degree it's a matter of personal taste, but many people and restaurants mistakenly think that any pasta can work with any sauce. That's not so. The type of sauce and the physiology of the noodle need to match.

Puréed, creamy, or clinging sauces are best served with such long, sleek pasta shapes as spaghetti, fettuccine, cappellini, or linguine—pastas that will allow the sauce to flow evenly over the face of the noodle.

Thinner, runnier sauces are better held by pastas that are twisted or curled. Those shapes trap liquid within their whorls, so that the sauce coats the pasta rather than the plate.

When a sauce is both thick and chunky, it is appropriate for any shape of pasta. It is viscous enough to coat long pastas, such as fettuccine and spaghetti, and its chunks are just right for filling the gaps in a shell or a spiral-shaped pasta.

Chunky sauces are best suited to pasta shapes that contain an opening. The nook of an elbow macaroni or the hollow of a shell pasta is just right for cradling a bit of shrimp or a morsel of sausage.

Many of the sauce recipes in this book specify a preferred pasta: long, curly, or shaped. The following are examples of each type.

- When a recipe calls for long pasta, use spaghetti, fettuccine, cappellini, linguine, or spirelli.

- When curly pasta is specified, use fusilli, rotelle, raddiatore, gemelini, or rigatoni.

- And when a recipe specifies shaped pasta, good choices are shells, elbows, ziti, penne, or wagon wheels.

Pasta Water

Salt is added to pasta water for flavoring, and no one seems to take issue with that. But there *is* some debate about adding oil. Today most chefs, including me, feel it is unnecessary, provided the pasta is stirred vigorously when it enters the water and again after the water returns to a boil, to be certain that the strands won't stick.

Pasta can stick when its starch expands in boiling water, causing a film of paste to form on its surfaces. Stirring keeps the pasta moving until a rolling boil can take over, and moving pasta doesn't have time to stick.

I've experienced sticking as a greater problem with some pasta brands and some shapes than with others. Small pastas, such as shells and elbows, have less tendency to stick than fettuccine or lasagna, because they have much less flat surface. Therefore flat pastas may require closer attention and a little more initial stirring than other shapes.

One other defense against sticking pasta is to be certain that your pasta pot is large enough. A pound of pasta needs a large, wide pot and at least four or five quarts of boiling water to move around in.

Grating Cheese

Some recipes end with a sprinkling (sometimes an optional sprinkling) of grated cheese, almost always one of the three common varieties—Parmesan, Romano, or Asiago. It's best if the cheese you use is freshly grated. Although this is not essential, you will usually get a better product if you buy grating cheeses in blocks and grate them as needed.

As important as fresh grating, however, is the nature of the cheese itself. Grating cheeses are quite dry, so their flavors are therefore concentrated. Whatever flavors they originally had or they developed during aging will be emphasized by the time the cheese is ready for market. If the milk was not fatty enough, the finished cheese will crumble. If excessive salt was used to hurry the drying, salt will dominate in the end. And if the cheese was not aged long enough to allow its acids to mellow properly, it will be coarse and acrid.

The best Parmesan is imported from Italy. It is called Parmigiano Reggiano and it is sold mostly in cheese stores, either in small blocks or grated. If you find a whole round, you will see it has a beige rind and the words *Parmigiano Reggiano* branded on the top, radiating from the center like the spokes of a wheel. This cheese is as dry as fine powder in the hand, but it melts into a silken, buttery glaze on the tongue. It is full-bodied but never harsh, and although it has a salty dimension, it is, overall, more dairy sweet than salty.

American Parmesan, on the other hand, especially the type sold grated and unrefrigerated, is a vastly inferior product. It smells spoiled, feels gritty, and tastes salty. It never melts and never becomes smooth, and I think it's a travesty that its commercial popularity has made it the cheese that most Americans envision when they think of Parmesan.

The only widely available, good-quality, domestically produced Parmesan that I have found is made by an Italian cheese-making firm in Wisconsin. Its brand name is Stella, and although I have experienced both good and bad batches, most of the time it is a perfectly good substitute when the imported cheese is unavailable. A trip to a cheese shop will yield good advice and more alternatives.

Romano is curded and aged the same way as Parmesan, except that it is made from sheep's milk rather than cow's milk. This gives Romano a sharper edge and less sweetness, a quality some people prefer and others find too harsh. Romano that's sold as Pecorino Romano is usually imported. (The word *Pecorino* refers to sheep's milk.)

Asiago (pronounced with a hard *g*) is a cow's-milk cheese that at one time was made from sheep's milk. Its flavor falls somewhere between that of Parmesan and Romano.

All dry cheeses store exceptionally well. Also, because of their low moisture content, they do not readily support bacterial growth and therefore can be stored for months without losing quality. Changing the cheese's wrapper will extend its shelf life even more.

Tomatoes and Tomato Products

Regardless of the season, you will be using tomatoes in your pasta sauces. At the height of summer, there is nothing better than a sauce made from fresh tomatoes. I have used both plum tomatoes and beefsteak varieties. Plum tomatoes have more pulp and less juice, but they often aren't as flavorful.

When fresh tomatoes aren't available or are substandard, you will get a better sauce by using canned tomatoes, which have been picked and packed at their height of ripeness. All canned tomatoes are cooked in the can. Minimally, they are heated to sterilize the contents. At most, they are boiled down to a paste. The more cooked a canned tomato is, the less it will resemble a fresh tomato and the more concentrated its flavor will be.

The available canned tomato products, from least to most cooked, are as follows.

Whole: Whole tomatoes in their own juice.

Diced (Recipe-Ready): A relatively new product, the same as whole tomatoes but cut up. I think they're a great idea; besides, when have you ever used a tomato whole in a recipe?

Crushed: The same as whole and diced but pulverized. The process causes a loss of water, which concentrates the pulp.

Purée: Crushed, cooked until thick, then sieved.

Paste: Concentrated purée, used only as a flavor booster. The best tomato paste I have ever found is packed in a tube by an Italian company under the Amore brand. It is very sweet, and best of all, the tube keeps any leftover paste fresh for months. No more throwing out half-used cans of tomato paste gone bad.

Sauce: A prepared recipe, not an unseasoned tomato product.

Stewed: Lightly cooked tomatoes with herbs, spices, and other vegetables.

Sun-dried: Dried tomatoes that can be bought unadorned, packed in oil, or worked into a paste. Anytime I use sun-dried tomatoes in this book, I use oil-cured sun-dried tomatoes. These come jarred, or you can cure them yourself by rehydrating dried tomatoes in water and soaking them in olive oil.

Roasted Peppers

Good-quality roasted red peppers are available in jars, and they'll be fine in these recipes. You can roast them yourself, whatever their color, although doing so will take some time. To roast your own bell peppers, place any number of peppers directly over the high flame of a gas burner or grill until they char on one side. Give the peppers a quarter turn and char again. Continue until the peppers are blackened all over. Place in a loosely closed paper bag and allow them to cool for 10 minutes. Peel by rubbing off the blackened skins with your fingers. Wash the skins from your fingers rather than washing the peppers, so that you don't wash away the peppers' flavorful oils.

Potatoes

One combination that I use frequently might strike you as unusual. Potatoes and pasta are great together. You boil the potatoes right along with dried pasta (they cook at the same rate), and as they cook, some of the starch from the potatoes coats the pasta, giving it a wonderful, creamy finish. Use any boiling, red-skin, new, or yellow-fleshed potato; Yukon Gold, one of the yellow-fleshed varieties, is the one I prefer.

Fish and Shellfish

Except for canned fish, all the fish called for in these pages are fresh fillets. The best way to choose fish is by smell. Perfectly fresh fish has no odor, except possibly the faint aroma of sea water. Any "fishy" odor is an indication of decay, which is why you should always ask to smell the fish you are about to buy. If the fish seller balks, you can bet something fishy is going on behind the counter.

Choose shrimp, scallops, and crabmeat by smell, but judge bivalve shellfish, like clams and mussels, by looking at their shells. When raw, clam and mussel shells must be clamped tight. If not, the clam or mussel will not be safe to eat and should be discarded. Mussels are especially perishable before cooking. Look over the shells carefully and buy about 10 percent more than you plan to serve to compensate for the duds you're almost certain to encounter.

Herbs

The recipes in these pages call for fresh herbs almost exclusively. That's not because I consider all fresh herbs inherently better than their dried counterparts. Far from it, fresh and dried herbs each have their place, but when time is of the essence, fresh herbs are the ones to use. Dried herbs just take too long to cook. They must be rehydrated to release their flavors, a process that usually takes too much time to meet this book's standards for preparation time.

A digression on fresh parsley: There are two kinds. Italian parsley, also called flat-leaf parsley, is the flavorful one. Curly parsley is the pretty one. There are not many hard and fast rules in my world view, but one of them is that you use flat-leaf parsley for cooking and curly parsley for garnishing.

Substituting one for the other won't ruin anything, but it certainly won't do your food any good.

Olive Oil

Almost without exception, every recipe in this book calls for olive oil. For sautéing, I usually use pure olive oil, while for flavoring I use extra-virgin. Extra-virgin oil comes from the first pressing of the fruit, which gives it the fullest olive flavor. It is also more expensive. "Pure" olive oil is made from a second pressing. Because much of an oil's aroma dissipates in the high heat of sautéing and because that aroma is the only reason to use an extra-virgin oil, I find sautéing in extra-virgin oil a bit wasteful. However, sometimes I'll do it to avoid using two different oils in the same recipe.

I am neither brand-loyal nor patriotic when it comes to olive oil. I shop price, not status or country of origin. I have found that the most expensive oils are frequently the most refined, making them brighter and clearer but also blander. The cheaper oils might be a bit cloudier or not as green, but often they are more aromatic, a quality that I prize.

Olives

Black olives are ripened green olives. They have more flavor, are softer, and are less salty than their green counterparts. When my recipes use olives, they are usually black, ripe olives. They can be any type—Niçoise, Mislinis, Kalamata—but not canned California olives. These ersatz black olives are not ripe and were never cured. They have none of the dark, earthy, fermented flavors that ripe olives should provide, and they will not give you good results.

Vegetables

You will find information about an individual vegetable in the recipe in which it is used. Of course, you should select the freshest and brightest produce possible for the best price, which usually means buying vegetables in season.

Seasonality is becoming increasingly obscure. International marketing brings corn to New York from South America in the middle of January and pineapples in July. Every local growing area, however, has its seasons, and being aware of them will help you purchase cheaper and better-quality produce. Vegetables that have traveled less distance to market can be harvested later without fear that they could be crushed or bruised from long transport.

Here's a brief seasonal list for the most common vegetables in North America.

Winter: beets, beet greens, celery root, collards, fennel, Jerusalem artichokes, kale, kohlrabi, broccoli rabe, winter squash

Spring: artichokes, asparagus, celery root, dandelion, peas, new potatoes

Summer: arugula, chard, tomatoes, plum tomatoes, corn, okra, peppers, zucchini, yellow squash

Fall: artichokes, beets, beet greens, celery root, collards, fennel, Jerusalem artichokes, okra, broccoli rabe, zucchini, yellow squash

Year round: beans, bean sprouts, broccoli, Brussels sprouts, cabbage, carrots, cauliflower, celery, cucumbers, endive, garlic, ginger, jicama, leeks, lemongrass, lettuce, mushrooms, onions, parsnips, potatoes, scallions, shallots, spinach, sweet potatoes, turnips, watercress

Cooking Techniques

Melting Cheese

Cheese is made from curds of milk protein, fat, and water. As a cheese starts to heat, its fat melts, causing the cheese to liquefy. If it gets even hotter, the protein tightens, eventually becoming taut enough to squeeze out the water. Soon the cheese will disintegrate into rubbery lumps floating in an oil-slicked, milky puddle.

As you can see, everything beyond the initial melting phase is a process of diminishing returns. That's why cheese is always added at the last minute—and usually off the heat.

Although all cheeses are subject to such destruction, some are more vulnerable than others. Low-fat cheeses, like mozzarella, have so much more protein than fat that they will not melt smoothly into a sauce no matter how careful you are. That's why mozzarella and provolone are usually layered with pasta and sauce in a casserole rather than used in making the sauce.

Higher-fat cheeses, like fontina and Cheddar, melt smoothly but have so little moisture that they cannot become saucelike without some added liquid. If the liquid has some fat of its own, like cream or a mix of oil and broth, the cheese will melt into it smoothly. But if the other liquid is very lean, the cheese will remain separate. To remedy this, cheese is frequently dusted with cornstarch to help thicken the sauce and absorb the melting fat.

Dry grating cheeses are used as a flavoring rather than as a base for a sauce. In order to coat pasta, they have to be combined with oil, broth, or milk.

Adjusting Sauce Texture

As you cook your way through these pages, you will discover that some of the tastiest sauces are relatively low in liquid, which may make it difficult to distribute the sauce evenly over the pasta. In those recipes I usually suggest adding a small amount of the pasta cooking water to the sauce before draining the pasta.

Similarly, unless a sauce is very thin or brothy, it helps most of the time to leave the cooked pasta slightly wet. A thin film of water helps the sauce flow over the pasta and keeps the pasta from absorbing too much sauce and becoming gummy.

Chapter 1

Tomato Sauces

Quick Fresh Tomato Sauce

Chili Tomato Sauce with Red Beans

Ginger Tomato Sauce

Roasted Pepper Tomato Sauce

Tomato Mint Vinaigrette

Tomato, Basil, and Cream

Tomato Sauce with Hot Pepper Vodka and Cream

Chipotle Tomato Sauce

Tomatoes, Tomatillos, and Green Olives

Lemon Tomato Sauce with Feta

Tomatoes are fruit, and like all fruit, their flavor is robust but their fiber is delicate. A few minutes of cooking is enough to release all that a tomato has to offer. Anything more begins a process of diminishing returns: What you gain in thickness and consistency, you rapidly lose in fragrance, sweetness, and subtlety.

The only flavor component that a tomato can retain during hours of cooking is acidity—the bane of all red sauces. To counteract acidity, cooks through the ages have loaded up their tomato sauces with caramelized onions, carrots, garlic, herbs, and sugar—anything sweet to kill what they saw as the unavoidable growth of acid. But what these cooks never realized was that the acid was not growing. Rather, the natural sweetness and perfume of the tomato, which had balanced its tang so perfectly when the fruit was raw, were being simmered away, irreversibly tipping the flavor scale to tartness.

1

All the doctoring that long-simmered sauces endure can be avoided by simply tasting the sauce and turning off the heat as soon as the flavor is right. What you get will be a bit thinner than a sauce that simmers all day, but so what? It will taste as fresh and sweet as the vine-ripened fruit from which it came. Consistency can be adjusted easily with a squirt of tomato paste (see information on tomato paste on page xviii) or a splash of cream.

Also, don't feel like you're cheating by substituting canned tomatoes for fresh when all that is available is tepid and pale. Because canned tomatoes are picked at their height of quality, they are often better than what you can buy. Just remember that these tomatoes have already been cooked in the can. They do not need the same amount of time over the heat to soften or release their juices.

A word about skinning and seeding tomatoes: *don't*. The reason tomatoes are usually skinned for long-simmered sauces is that the skin doesn't soften along with the pulp, resulting in tiny shards of skin in an otherwise silken purée. But when sauces are cooked quickly, the tomato flesh keeps its texture and stays attached to its skin. The results are chunkier, and the presence of the tomato skin is unnoticeable.

The drawback of removing the seeds from tomatoes is that those seeds are surrounded by flavorful juices that will inevitably be thrown out with the seeds. To my mind, ridding a sauce of a few seeds is not worth this massive loss of flavor and nutrition.

Quick Fresh Tomato Sauce

**Makes
4 servings**

This straightforward recipe transports the Old World mainstay of tomato sauce made from scratch into the fast-paced contemporary kitchen. Without the hours of simmering, poking, and skimming, you'll get an all-purpose sauce full of vegetable flavor and balanced with herbs, garlic, and a hint of hot pepper.

1 pound pasta, any type

2 tablespoons olive oil

1 large onion, chopped

2 cloves garlic, minced

1 small dried chili pepper

12 fresh plum tomatoes, stemmed and chopped, or one 28-ounce can whole tomatoes, drained and coarsely chopped

1 tablespoon tomato paste

Salt and freshly ground black pepper to taste

8 fresh basil leaves, chopped

Freshly grated Parmesan or Romano cheese (optional)

Bring a large pot of lightly salted water to a boil. Add the pasta and stir a few times to ensure that the pasta does not stick to itself. Boil vigorously for the time recommended on the pasta package or until the pasta is tender.

While the pasta cooks, heat the oil in a medium skillet over medium-high heat, add the onion, and cook until softened, about 2 minutes. Add the garlic, chili pepper, and tomatoes and cook until the tomatoes bubble vigorously, about 4 minutes. Stir in the tomato paste, season with salt and pepper, stir in the basil, and heat for 1 more minute. Remove the chili pepper.

Drain the pasta and toss it with the sauce in a serving bowl. Serve with grated cheese if desired.

Chili Tomato Sauce with Red Beans

**Makes
4 servings**

Think of this as a cowboy version of pasta e fagioli, *or chili for spaghetti. Either way, the color and flavor in this sauce are purely American. And the beans and pasta form a complete protein. This dish is especially convenient made with canned beans, but if you have some home-cooked beans left over from another recipe, their meaty texture will provide an even better counterpoint to the pasta.*

---

1 pound shaped pasta, such as wagon wheels or shells

2 tablespoons olive oil

1 large onion, chopped

1 green bell pepper, stemmed, seeded, and cut in medium dice

2 cloves garlic, minced

1 tablespoon chili powder

2 teaspoons ground cumin

1/4 teaspoon dried oregano

12 fresh plum tomatoes, stemmed and chopped, or one 28-ounce can whole tomatoes, drained and coarsely chopped, or two 14-ounce cans diced tomatoes

1 tablespoon tomato paste

1 teaspoon sugar

Salt and freshly ground black pepper to taste

1 cup canned red kidney beans, drained and washed

1/2 cup (2 ounces) shredded Cheddar cheese (optional)

Bring a large pot of lightly salted water to a boil. Add the pasta and stir a few times to ensure that the pasta does not stick to itself. Boil vigorously for the time recommended on the pasta package or until the pasta is tender.

While the pasta cooks, heat the oil in a medium skillet over medium-high heat, add the onion and bell pepper, and cook until softened, about 2 minutes. Add the garlic, chili powder, cumin, oregano, and tomatoes and cook until the tomatoes bubble vigorously, about 4 minutes. Stir in the tomato paste and the sugar, season with salt and pepper, stir in the beans, and simmer 2 more minutes.

Drain the pasta and toss it in a serving bowl with the sauce and, if desired, the cheese.

Ginger Tomato Sauce

**Makes
4 servings**

I know it's unusual, but I have come to love the combination of ginger and tomato. I use it repeatedly in salsa, tomato soup, and gingerbread, and this sauce is one of my favorites. The ginger lends the same spark to the tomato as does a pinch of hot pepper, but with more aroma and sweetness. While you're at it, make a double batch of this sauce and use the extra on grilled fish, baked chicken, or as a poaching liquid for eggs.

---

1 pound pasta, any type

2 tablespoons olive oil

1 large onion, chopped

2 tablespoons finely chopped fresh ginger

2 cloves garlic, minced

12 fresh plum tomatoes, stemmed and chopped, or one 28-ounce can whole tomatoes, drained and coarsely chopped, or two 14-ounce cans diced tomatoes

1 tablespoon tomato paste

Salt and freshly ground black pepper to taste

4 whole scallions, thinly sliced

Bring a large pot of lightly salted water to a boil. Add the pasta and stir a few times to ensure that the pasta does not stick to itself. Boil vigorously for the time recommended on the pasta package or until the pasta is tender.

While the pasta cooks, heat the oil in a medium skillet over medium-high heat, add the onion and ginger, and cook until the onion softens, about 2 minutes. Add the garlic and tomatoes and cook until the tomatoes bubble vigorously, about 4 minutes. Stir in the tomato paste, season with salt and pepper, stir in the scallions, and cook for 1 more minute.

Drain the pasta and toss it with the sauce in a serving bowl.

Roasted Pepper Tomato Sauce

**Makes
4 servings**

Roasted red peppers give this sauce a char-cooked redolence and a brilliant crimson color. Their intense aroma and robust flavor are instantly imparted to the sauce, so it's less essential that the tomatoes be as perfectly ripe as in some other tomato sauces. Although homemade roasted peppers are fuller-flavored than their commercially prepared counterparts, roasted peppers from a jar give fine results.

---

1 pound pasta, any type

2 tablespoons extra-virgin olive oil

1 large onion, chopped

One 7-ounce jar roasted red bell peppers, cut in medium dice, or 2 large roasted red bell peppers (page xix), stemmed, seeded, and cut in medium dice

2 cloves garlic, minced

1 dried chili pepper

12 fresh plum tomatoes, stemmed and chopped, or one 28-ounce can whole tomatoes, drained and coarsely chopped, or two 14-ounce cans diced tomatoes

Salt and freshly ground black pepper to taste

12 fresh basil leaves, chopped

Freshly grated Parmesan or Romano cheese (optional)

Bring a large pot of lightly salted water to a boil. Add the pasta and stir a few times to ensure that the pasta does not stick to itself. Boil vigorously for the time recommended on the pasta package or until the pasta is tender.

While the pasta cooks, heat the oil in a medium skillet over medium-high heat, add the onion, and cook until softened, about 2 minutes. Add the roasted peppers, garlic, chili pepper, and tomatoes and cook until the tomatoes bubble vigorously, about 4 minutes. Season with salt and pepper, stir in the basil, and cook for 1 more minute. Remove the chili pepper.

Drain the pasta and toss it with the sauce in a serving bowl. Serve with grated cheese if desired.

Tomato Mint Vinaigrette

Makes 4 servings

Canned crushed tomatoes provide the perfect sweet-tart, mildly thickened base for this vinaigrette sauce. In most vinaigrettes, the amounts of oil and vinegar determine the amount of the sauce. But in this recipe, the bulk of the sauce is pure tomato, while the vinegar and oil are just flavorings, balanced and enhanced by the mentholated sweetness of a bunch of fresh mint.

1 pound pasta, any type
One 28-ounce can crushed tomatoes
1 bunch mint leaves, finely chopped
2 cloves garlic, minced

1/4 cup extra-virgin olive oil
1 tablespoon balsamic vinegar
3 to 4 ounces feta or fresh chèvre, in small
   pieces (optional)

Bring a large pot of lightly salted water to a boil. Add the pasta and stir a few times to ensure that the pasta does not stick to itself. Boil vigorously for the time recommended on the pasta package or until the pasta is tender.

While the pasta cooks, simmer the tomatoes, stirring often, in a heavy 2- or 3-quart saucepan over medium-high heat until slightly thickened, about 5 minutes. Stir in the mint and garlic and simmer for another 2 minutes. Remove from the heat and stir in the olive oil and the vinegar.

Drain the pasta and toss it with the sauce in a serving bowl. Serve with cheese if desired.

Tomato, Basil, and Cream

**Makes
4 servings**

*This lightly cooked tomato sauce is enriched with cream, an addition that
requires care. Cream is an emulsion of protein, water, and milk fat. The fat will
melt, making the sauce smoother and richer, while the protein congeals, thickening the sauce. If the protein gets too firm, the sauce will split. This potential
problem is exacerbated by heat and acid—two things a simmering tomato
sauce has in spades. So watch carefully as you mix in the cream. As soon as the
sauce starts to thicken, remove it from the heat. And be on guard. It could take
10 seconds or a minute; older cream sets up faster and has a greater chance of
splitting than very fresh cream.*

---

1 pound long pasta, such as fettuccine or
   spaghetti
16 large ripe plum tomatoes
2 tablespoons extra-virgin olive oil
2 cloves garlic, minced

1 tablespoon tomato paste
1/3 cup heavy cream
Salt and freshly ground black pepper to taste
24 fresh basil leaves, torn or coarsely
   chopped

Bring a large pot of lightly salted water to a boil. Add the pasta and stir a few
times to ensure that the pasta does not stick to itself. Boil vigorously for the
time recommended on the pasta package or until the pasta is tender.

While the pasta cooks, remove and discard the stem ends from the tomatoes and chop the tomatoes into small pieces. Heat the oil in a large skillet over
medium-high heat. Add the garlic and stir briskly. Immediately add the tomatoes, all of their juices, and the tomato paste and cook until the tomatoes
bubble vigorously, about 4 minutes. Stir in the cream and simmer until the
sauce thickens slightly, about 1 minute, but maybe less (see comment above).
Stir in the salt, pepper, and basil.

Drain the pasta and toss it with the sauce in a serving bowl.

Tomato Sauce with Hot Pepper Vodka and Cream

Usually, spirits are added to sauces early on to ensure that they cook long enough to boil off the alcohol. But not here. In this sauce, a shot of pepper vodka is thrown in at the last possible minute, giving the sauce a double jolt of heat. Follow the same guidelines for adding the cream as described in the comment preceding the previous recipe. And skip this recipe if you're avoiding alcohol.

---

1 pound long pasta, such as fettuccine or
    spaghetti

16 large plum tomatoes

2 tablespoons olive oil

2 cloves garlic, minced

1 tablespoon tomato paste

1/3 cup heavy cream

Salt and freshly ground black pepper to taste

2 tablespoons chopped fresh Italian (flat-leaf)
    parsley

2 tablespoons pepper vodka (see note below)

Bring a large pot of lightly salted water to a boil. Add the pasta and stir a few times to ensure that the pasta does not stick to itself. Boil vigorously for the time recommended on the pasta package or until the pasta is tender.

While the pasta cooks, remove and discard the stem ends from the tomatoes and chop the tomatoes into small pieces. Heat the oil in a large skillet over medium-high heat, add the garlic, and stir briskly. Immediately add the tomatoes, all their juices, and the tomato paste and cook until the tomatoes bubble vigorously, about 4 minutes. Stir in the cream and simmer until the sauce thickens slightly, about a minute but maybe much less. Remove from the heat and stir in the salt, pepper, parsley, and vodka.

Drain the pasta and toss it with the sauce in a serving bowl.

Note: *Pepper vodka is one of many flavored vodkas now commonly available. You can make your own by soaking 1 teaspoon of crushed red pepper flakes in 1 cup of vodka overnight.*

Chipotle Tomato Sauce

**Makes
4 servings**

Chipotles are smoked dried jalapeño peppers. They're less fiery than fresh jalapeños but they make up for it with an abundance of smoky aroma. Their flavor is unique and well worth searching out. Chipotles are available in many supermarkets and any place where dried chili peppers are sold. Because chipotles are dried, they do not need refrigeration and will keep for several months in a kitchen cabinet, so stock up when you find them.

---

1 pound shaped pasta, such as wagon wheels or shells

2 tablespoons olive oil

1 large onion, chopped

2 cloves garlic, minced

2 chipotle peppers, stemmed, seeded, and finely chopped (see note below)

2 teaspoons ground cumin

1/4 teaspoon dried oregano

12 fresh plum tomatoes, stemmed and chopped, or one 28-ounce can whole tomatoes, drained and coarsely chopped, or two 14-ounce cans diced tomatoes

1 tablespoon tomato paste

1 teaspoon sugar

Salt and freshly ground black pepper to taste

2 tablespoons chopped fresh cilantro

Bring a large pot of lightly salted water to a boil. Add the pasta and stir a few times to ensure that the pasta does not stick to itself. Boil vigorously for the time recommended on the pasta package or until the pasta is tender.

While the pasta cooks, heat the oil in a medium skillet over medium-high heat, add the onion, and cook until softened, about 2 minutes. Add the garlic, chipotle, cumin, oregano, and tomatoes and cook until the tomatoes bubble vigorously, about 4 minutes. Stir in the tomato paste and the sugar, season with salt and pepper, stir in the cilantro, and simmer 2 more minutes.

Drain the pasta and toss it with the sauce in a serving bowl.

Note: *It is easiest to chop the chipotle peppers in a mini chopper or mini food processor. Start by cutting or breaking the pepper into small pieces and then grind finely.*

Tomatoes, Tomatillos, and Green Olives

Makes 4 servings

Even though you may have no idea what a tomatillo looks or tastes like, you almost certainly have eaten one, for tomatillos are the vegetable of choice for making green salsa. Once they're peeled of their papery skins, they look like large, pale, green cherry tomatoes. Although you can serve tomatillos raw, they are at their best when cooked. That's when they reveal a delicate lemony-herbal flavor and a natural thickening ability.

---

1 pound pasta, any shape

2 tablespoons olive oil

1/2 medium onion, chopped

1 jalapeño pepper, stemmed, seeded, and cut in fine dice

6 plum tomatoes, stemmed and cut in medium dice

6 tomatillos, husked and cut in medium dice

2 sprigs fresh oregano leaves, chopped (about 1 tablespoon)

1/2 cup water

12 pitted green olives, coarsely chopped

Salt and freshly ground black pepper to taste

1 tablespoon extra-virgin olive oil

Bring a large pot of lightly salted water to a boil. Add the pasta and stir a few times to ensure that the pasta does not stick to itself. Boil vigorously for the time recommended on the pasta package or until the pasta is tender.

While the pasta cooks, heat the olive oil in a medium skillet over medium-high heat, add the onion and jalapeño, and cook until the onion softens, about 2 minutes. Add the tomatoes, tomatillos, and oregano and cook for 1 minute. Add the water and simmer until the tomatoes soften and most of the water is gone, about 4 minutes. Stir in the olives, salt, pepper, and olive oil.

Drain the pasta and toss it with the sauce in a serving bowl.

Lemon Tomato Sauce with Feta

Although many cooks do everything in their power to eliminate acid in their tomato sauces, I find that a little lemon juice, properly placed, can work wonders. It brings out the flavor of the tomato and adds its own clean spark. In this recipe, fresh oregano gives the combination depth and fresh feta cheese gives it a dairy richness, lending the impression of cream with only a fraction of its fat.

---

1 pound curly pasta, such as fusilli or rotelle

1 tablespoon olive oil

1/2 medium onion, chopped

1 clove garlic, minced

4 large tomatoes, stemmed and chopped

Pinch of cayenne pepper

Salt and freshly ground black pepper to taste

2 teaspoons chopped fresh oregano or 2 tablespoons chopped fresh basil

Juice of 1 lemon

6 ounces feta cheese, crumbled

Bring a large pot of lightly salted water to a boil. Add the pasta and stir a few times to ensure that the pasta does not stick to itself. Boil vigorously for the time recommended on the pasta package or until the pasta is tender.

While the pasta cooks, heat the olive oil in a medium skillet over medium-high heat and cook the onion in the oil until softened, about 2 minutes. Add the garlic and tomatoes and cook until the tomatoes bubble vigorously, about 4 minutes. Season with cayenne, salt, and pepper, toss in the chopped herbs, and cook another minute. Remove from the heat and add the lemon juice.

Drain the pasta and toss it with the sauce and the feta cheese in a serving bowl.

Chapter 2

Herb Sauces

Parsley, Garlic, and Cheese Sauce

Basil and Prosciutto Sauce

Lemon Basil Pesto

Smoky Almond Pesto

Rosemary and Sage Aïoli

Fennel, Shrimp, and Saffron Sauce

Watercress, Black Pepper, and Chèvre Sauce

Fines Herbes and Capers Sauce

Spicy Herbed Mushroom Sauce

Dill and Potato Sauce

It is said that ancient mariners, approaching Italy's northwest coast, sniffed their way ashore, guided by the anise scent of basil that still fills the fields surrounding Genoa. The impact of fresh herbs on plain pasta works the same way, fusing with our senses even before we take a taste.

Pestos, wine sauces, butter sauces, or simple tosses of chopped herbs and garlic spread through a plate of noodles, instantly transforming the aroma, color, texture, and flavor of the food with minimal cooking.

The sauces in this chapter concentrate exclusively on fresh herbs. Unlike dried seasoning, fresh herbs require no cooking. They release their flavors immediately, making them perfect for infusing flavor into a quick or uncooked sauce. Even when herb sauces call for cooking, they don't take much. Think of fresh herbs as you would other leafy vegetables. They are best cooked quickly, for once the leaf is wilted, the herb is cooked. Additional heat will only dissipate an herb's flavor and destroy its color.

This is why fresh herbs are added near the end of sauce making. Even when an herb is the main ingredient, it will usually join the recipe after everything else has had its chance to soften and bloom, so that the aroma of the herb reaches its peak after it comes off the heat, just when the sauce is blending with the pasta and is on its way toward the mouth.

Pesto is probably the most famous of all herb pasta sauces. Made from ground pine nuts, garlic, basil, and cheese, it is never cooked, relying exclusively on chopping and the subtle heat of hot pasta to give it a sauce-like consistency and to release its flavor. That flavor is one of the most intense in all of sauce making—and one that is very easy to manipulate into numerous variations. Oregano and walnuts, for example, make a potent pesto, perfect for grilled meats or meat-filled pastas. This chapter contains two nontraditional pestos. One is light and bright and replaces the pine nuts with lower fat and more highly flavored lemon zest. The other goes for richer, more pungent flavor by starting with a base of Smokehouse almonds.

Parsley, Garlic, and Cheese Sauce

**Makes
4 servings**

There are two parsleys. Curly parsley is for garnish. Flat-leaf, or Italian, parsley is the one for cooking. It has a broad, maple-shaped leaf, a deep green color, and a flavor full of garden freshness and spice. Unlike more pungent herbs, parsley can be used in abundance, allowing us to inundate plain pasta with brilliant emerald green and still permit a balance of freshly grated cheese, garlic, and olive oil to shine through.

1 pound pasta, any shape

6 tablespoons extra-virgin olive oil

2 cloves garlic, minced

1 cup chopped fresh Italian (flat-leaf) parsley

Salt and freshly ground black pepper to taste

1/3 cup freshly grated Romano cheese

Bring a large pot of lightly salted water to a boil. Add the pasta and stir a few times to ensure that the pasta does not stick to itself. Boil vigorously for the time recommended on the pasta package or until the pasta is tender.

While the pasta cooks, combine the oil, garlic, parsley, salt, pepper, and cheese in a serving bowl. Drain the pasta and toss it in the bowl with the parsley mixture.

Basil and Prosciutto Sauce

**Makes
4 servings**

Italians don't smoke their meats, but that doesn't keep them from producing some of the best hams in the world. Prosciutto di Parma is the one most commonly available in America. Prosciutto is not boiled or baked like most hams. Rather, it is "cooked" by exposure to salt, resulting in an intense concentration of sweet, meaty flavor. Real prosciutto is quite expensive, but a little bit goes a long way. Domestic prosciutto is much cheaper, but these hams are very salty and often quite stringy, making a few ounces of imported prosciutto a better buy than a pound of the budget brand.

---

1 pound shaped pasta, such as penne or
    wagon wheels

6 tablespoons olive oil

1 small bunch basil leaves (about 2 cups),
    washed, dried, and chopped

2 cloves garlic, minced

2 ounces imported prosciutto, finely chopped

1 large tomato, stemmed and diced

Pinch of crushed red pepper flakes

Salt and freshly ground black pepper to taste

Bring a large pot of lightly salted water to a boil. Add the pasta and stir a few times to ensure that the pasta does not stick to itself. Boil vigorously for the time recommended on the pasta package or until the pasta is tender.

While the pasta cooks, combine the oil, basil, garlic, prosciutto, tomato, red pepper flakes, salt, and pepper in a serving bowl.

Drain the pasta and toss it in the bowl with the basil mixture.

Lemon Basil Pesto

**Makes
4 servings**

*Lemon and basil are wondrous together, but the pairing doesn't work in pesto.
The problem is acid. Citric acid turns the basil a drab color, and its tartness
gives Parmesan cheese a spoiled taste. Enter zest. Lemon zest, the yellow skin of
the peel, is bursting with lemon flavor, but since it contains lemon oil rather
than citric acid, it has all the flavor assets but none of the caustic problems.*

1 pound pasta, any shape
Finely grated zest of 1 lemon
1 small bunch basil leaves (about 2 cups),
 washed and dried

1 large clove garlic, halved
2 tablespoons freshly grated Parmesan cheese
5 tablespoons olive oil
Salt and freshly ground black pepper to taste

Bring a large pot of lightly salted water to a boil. Add the pasta and stir a few
times to ensure that the pasta does not stick to itself. Boil vigorously for the
time recommended on the pasta package or until the pasta is tender.

While the pasta cooks, combine the lemon zest, basil, and garlic in the
work bowl of a food processor and process until finely chopped. Add the
cheese, oil, salt, and pepper and process until the mixture has become a rough
paste. Transfer the mixture to a serving bowl and stir $\frac{1}{2}$ cup of the pasta water
into the pesto.

Drain the pasta and toss it in the bowl with the sauce. Adjust the seasoning.

Smoky Almond Pesto

**Makes
4 servings**

Pesto, the aromatic basil paste from Genoa, is most typically made with raw pine nuts. In this recipe, smoke-cured almonds take their place, compounding the intoxicating fragrance of basil with the sweet scent of hickory smoke and toasted almonds.

1 pound pasta, any shape

1 clove garlic

⅓ cup Smokehouse almonds

1 small bunch basil leaves (about 2 cups),
    washed and dried

6 tablespoons extra-virgin olive oil

2 tablespoons freshly grated Parmesan cheese

Salt and freshly ground black pepper to taste

Bring a large pot of lightly salted water to a boil. Add the pasta and stir a few times to ensure that the pasta does not stick to itself. Boil vigorously for the time recommended on the pasta package or until the pasta is tender.

While the pasta cooks, finely chop the garlic, almonds, and basil with a knife or in a food processor or blender. Transfer the mixture to a serving bowl and stir in the oil, cheese, salt, and pepper.

Drain the pasta and toss it in the bowl with the pesto.

Rosemary and Sage Aïoli

Makes 4 servings

Aïoli, the creamy garlic mayonnaise of the Riviera, is typically used to enrich stews and soups, as a spread, and as a dip. In this recipe, a lot of fresh herbs help it become an intoxicating pasta sauce. This preparation uses uncooked egg yolk, and that always requires special attention to the eggs, which must be the best quality possible. If you want to make this sauce without the yolk, its flavor will be unchanged, but the resulting sauce will lack the creaminess and richness of the original.

1 pound pasta, any shape
$1/3$ cup fresh rosemary leaves
$1/3$ cup fresh sage leaves
2 cloves garlic
2 tablespoons seasoned bread crumbs

1 egg yolk
Juice of 1 medium lemon
7 tablespoons olive oil
Salt and freshly ground black pepper to taste

Bring a large pot of lightly salted water to a boil. Add the pasta and stir a few times to ensure that the pasta does not stick to itself. Boil vigorously for the time recommended on the pasta package or until the pasta is tender.

While the pasta cooks, finely chop the rosemary, sage, and garlic in a food processor. Add the bread crumbs, egg yolk, and lemon juice and purée. With the processor on, slowly add the oil until the mixture is homogeneous. Season with salt and pepper.

Drain the pasta and toss it with the sauce in a serving bowl.

Fennel, Shrimp, and Saffron Sauce

**Makes
4 servings**

This sauce exploits the licorice-like flavor of fennel in two forms. Fresh fennel stalks are sautéed with onion and bolstered with ground fennel seed after they are softened. Fennel is a favorite foil for seafood in many Mediterranean cuisines; here it is gilded, in the tradition of Provence, with a golden glow of saffron.

1/4 teaspoon saffron threads

1 cup dry white wine

1 pound pasta, any shape

1 tablespoon olive oil

1 medium onion, chopped

1 rib fennel, peeled and cut in medium dice

1 clove garlic, minced

1 teaspoon fennel seed, ground

1/2 pound large (26–30 count) shrimp, peeled, deveined, and halved lengthwise

4 tablespoons (1/2 stick) unsalted butter

Salt and freshly ground black pepper to taste

Crumble the saffron into the wine and set aside.

Bring a large pot of lightly salted water to a boil. Add the pasta and stir a few times to ensure that the pasta does not stick to itself. Boil vigorously for the time recommended on the pasta package or until the pasta is tender.

While the pasta cooks, heat the oil in a nonstick skillet over medium-high heat, add the onion and fennel, and cook until the vegetables soften, about 2 minutes, stirring often. Add the garlic and fennel seed and cook another 30 seconds. Add the saffron-wine mixture and boil vigorously until the liquid reduces to about 1/4 cup, about 4 minutes. Add the shrimp and simmer for 30 seconds. Remove from the heat and mix in the butter. Season with salt and pepper.

Drain the pasta and toss it with the sauce in a serving bowl.

Watercress, Black Pepper, and Chèvre Sauce

Watercress is not usually thought of as an herb, but its peppery spice is certainly assertive enough to qualify. This recipe embellishes that flavor with a hefty dose of cracked black pepper and is tempered by the creamy balm of goat cheese. Make sure to trim off all the stems from the watercress; they can turn the sauce bitter as it sits.

1 pound pasta, any shape
1 bunch watercress leaves, finely chopped
1 clove garlic, finely chopped
5 ounces fresh chèvre (goat cheese), crumbled

1 teaspoon coarsely ground black
  peppercorns
Salt to taste

Bring a large pot of lightly salted water to a boil. Add the pasta and stir a few times to ensure that the pasta does not stick to itself. Boil vigorously for the time recommended on the pasta package or until the pasta is tender.

While the pasta cooks, combine the watercress, garlic, chèvre, pepper, and salt in a serving bowl. Stir in ½ cup of the pasta water.

Drain the pasta and toss it in the bowl with the chèvre mixture.

Fines Herbes and Capers Sauce

**Makes
4 servings**

The subtle perfume of fines herbes is enlivened with the magical spark of the pickled flower bud called the caper. These tiny beads of flavor come from a trailing vine that has been cultivated in the Mediterranean since ancient times. You can buy them pickled in dry salt or brine. I prefer the briny ones, and I don't rinse them, although I know many people who do. The best capers are the smallest, which are sold as "nonpareil" capers. If you can find only the larger ones, chop them a bit before using. Don't worry if you have an opened jar of capers in your refrigerator. They will not spoil, and they'll provide you with an instantly flavorful, fat-free resource for sautéed meats, scrambled eggs, and boiled vegetables.

---

1 pound pasta, any shape

1 medium shallot, finely chopped

1 clove garlic, minced

1 teaspoon olive oil

1/2 cup dry white wine

1/4 cup chopped fresh Italian (flat-leaf) parsley

1/4 cup chopped fresh savory, chervil, or
   additional parsley

2 teaspoons chopped fresh sage or rosemary

1/4 cup capers

4 tablespoons (1/2 stick) butter

Salt and freshly ground black pepper to taste

1/4 cup freshly grated Parmesan or Romano
   cheese (optional)

Bring a large pot of lightly salted water to a boil. Add the pasta and stir a few times to ensure that the pasta does not stick to itself. Boil vigorously for the time recommended on the pasta package or until the pasta is tender.

While the pasta cooks, combine the shallot, garlic, and oil in a medium nonstick skillet and sauté, stirring frequently, over medium-high heat for 1 minute, until the shallot has softened. Add the wine and boil until it has reduced to 3 tablespoons. Add the herbs, stir to combine, and cook for

30 seconds. Add the capers and cook for another minute. Remove from the heat and stir in the butter. Season with salt and pepper.

Drain the pasta and toss it in a serving bowl with the sauce and, if desired, the cheese.

Spicy Herbed Mushroom Sauce

**Makes
4 servings**

It doesn't seem right that mushrooms are such a natural complement to pasta. The two just have too much in common—a toothsome texture, a mild flavor that easily takes on whatever it is paired with, nearly identical colors. For whatever reason, it works, and this sauce is a prime example. It enlivens the classic couple with a hit of red pepper, some sweet bits of tomato, and some parsley. The preparation is quick and easy and the results are pure comfort food.

1 pound shaped pasta, such as orecchiette or medium shells

2 tablespoons olive oil

1/2 medium onion, finely chopped

1 clove garlic, minced

Pinch of crushed red pepper flakes

1/2 pound small mushrooms, cleaned, stemmed, and sliced

1/3 cup chopped fresh Italian (flat-leaf) parsley

2 large plum tomatoes, stemmed and diced

Bring a large pot of lightly salted water to a boil. Add the pasta and stir a few times to ensure that the pasta does not stick to itself. Boil vigorously for the time recommended on the pasta package or until the pasta is tender.

While the pasta cooks, heat the oil in a large skillet over medium-high heat, add the onion, and cook until softened, about 2 minutes. Add the garlic and red pepper flakes and stir to combine. Add the mushrooms, reduce the heat to medium, and cook until the mushrooms lose their raw look, about 3 minutes. Add the parsley and tomatoes and cook a few minutes more, until the tomatoes soften. Stir in 1/2 cup of the pasta water.

Drain the pasta and toss it with the sauce in a serving bowl.

Dill and Potato Sauce

**Makes
4 servings**

Cooking pasta and vegetables together is a well-known time-saver. In this recipe, potatoes are added with the pasta, and provided the potatoes are cut to the right size (about 1-inch cubes), they will cook perfectly in the same time it takes to cook dried pasta. Besides boosting the nutrition and flavor of the dish, the potatoes lend a rich, creamy texture to the sauce without adding any fat.

1 pound shaped pasta, such as shells or
   penne
1 pound red-skin or yellow-flesh potatoes,
   peeled and cut in 1-inch dice
1/4 cup extra-virgin olive oil
2 shallots, finely chopped

2 tablespoons chopped fresh dill
1 clove garlic, minced
Salt and freshly ground black pepper to taste
3 tablespoons freshly grated Romano cheese

Bring a large pot of lightly salted water to a boil. Add the pasta and the potatoes and stir a few times to ensure that the pasta does not stick to itself. Boil vigorously for the time recommended on the pasta package or until the pasta is tender.

While the pasta cooks, combine the oil, shallots, and dill in a medium skillet and cook over medium heat until the shallots soften, about 1 minute. Add the garlic, cook another minute, and season with salt and pepper.

Drain the pasta and potatoes and toss them with the shallot mixture and the cheese in a serving bowl.

Chapter 3

Dry Sauces

Tomato and Olive Sauce

Roasted Pepper and Anchovy Sauce

Smoky Corn and Rosemary Sauce

Tuna, Hazelnut, and Garlic Sauce

Marinated Artichoke and Feta Sauce

Roquefort, Walnut, and Fennel Sauce

Tomato, Basil, and Chèvre Sauce

Pumpkin Seed and Chili Pesto

Mushroom, Sweet Vinegar, and Garlic Sauce

Peas and Prosciutto Sauce

*A**glio e olio*, the simplest of all Italian pasta sauces, is nothing more than fresh garlic, fragrant olive oil, and a handful of grated cheese. It requires less than a minute of cooking, yields less than a cup of sauce, and practically disappears once it's on the pasta. Until you taste it, that is.

Whatever may be missing in fluid is made up for in a rush of flavor, for the very lack of moisture is what makes what I call dry sauces taste so good. Technically, none of these sauces are truly dry. They all have *some* fluid, usually oil or the moisture from vegetables, to help them flow over the noodles.

What they are missing is a lot of water—the stuff that turns tomatoes into sauce or makes milk or cream pourable. In many ways, this makes things easier. Water has no flavor, and too much of it will make a sauce thin. Getting rid of excess water is the reason traditional pasta sauces take so long to cook.

But dry sauces contain nothing to dilute flavors. A few seconds over a flame is all they need to realize their potential, whether they're made from fresh tomatoes and grated cheese, rosemary and ham, or walnuts and Roquefort.

Dry sauces rely on precooked, cured, and marinated ingredients, making them instantly flavorful and easy. Hours of simmering can do nothing to increase the flavor of olives or ham or roasted peppers. Chopped nuts and seeds coat pasta with rich oils and natural sweetness after just a brief toasting; combined with a little chopped garlic or hot pepper, they become an instant sauce.

I take advantage of good-quality canned goods—products such as oil-packed anchovies and tuna, oil-cured sun-dried tomatoes, pickled olives, artichoke hearts, and chilies—for dry sauces. Teaming these ingredients with a flavorful creamy cheese, such as gorgonzola or feta, can produce a sauce that not only is ready to go in minutes but bypasses cooking altogether. (For additional uncooked sauces, see Chapter 9 on page 101.)

Certain vegetables lend themselves well to dry treatments. Mushrooms release just enough moisture in cooking to qualify as saucy and at the same time intensify in flavor without losing their shape. When finely chopped, the celery-like stalks of fennel infuse a quickly sautéed sauce with a pungent anise perfume that makes additional liquid superfluous. Minced garlic, pepper, and tomato melt effortlessly into a sauce that needs only olive oil and freshly grated cheese to transform plain pasta into a flavor-packed *tour de force*.

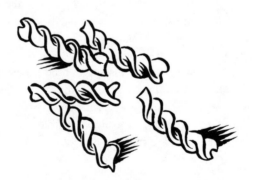

Tomato and Olive Sauce

**Makes
4 servings**

Don't even bother making this sauce with those tepid, genetically engineered hothouse tomatoes. Because the tomatoes aren't cooked, only perfectly ripe tomatoes can assure you garden-fresh results. You'll be rewarded with a quick, stunning sauce that percolates with flavor.

---

1 pound shaped pasta, such as shells or ziti

8 very ripe plum tomatoes

2 cloves garlic, minced

12 black olives (Niçoise, Kalamata, Mislinis), pitted and finely chopped

Pinch of crushed red pepper flakes

¼ cup chopped fresh Italian (flat-leaf) parsley

6 tablespoons extra-virgin olive oil

5 tablespoons freshly grated Parmesan cheese

Salt and freshly ground black pepper to taste

Bring a large pot of lightly salted water to a boil. Add the pasta and stir a few times to ensure that the pasta does not stick to itself. Boil vigorously for the time recommended on the pasta package or until the pasta is tender.

While the pasta cooks, cut and discard the stem ends from the tomatoes and chop the tomatoes into bite-size pieces. In a serving bowl, toss the tomatoes with the garlic, olives, red pepper flakes, parsley, and olive oil.

Drain the pasta and toss it in the bowl with the sauce. Add the cheese, salt, and pepper.

Roasted Pepper and Anchovy Sauce

**Makes
4 servings**

The acrid char and sweet fruit of roasted red peppers make a natural mate for the salt-drenched succulence of anchovies. In this dish, both ingredients are cut into thin strips to match the ribbon shape of the pasta. A simple vinaigrette of olive oil, lemon juice, and basil enhances the flavors of both fish and fruit and helps disperse them evenly over the strands of noodles.

---

1 pound long pasta, such as fettuccine or linguine

One 7-ounce jar roasted peppers, cut in strips, or 3 roasted red bell peppers (see page xix), stemmed, seeded, and cut in strips

2 cloves garlic, minced

12 anchovy fillets packed in olive oil, drained, and cut in thin strips

¹/₄ cup extra-virgin olive oil

Juice of ¹/₂ medium lemon

¹/₄ cup chopped fresh basil or fresh Italian (flat-leaf) parsley

¹/₄ cup freshly grated Parmesan or Romano cheese, or a combination

Salt and freshly ground black pepper to taste

Bring a large pot of lightly salted water to a boil. Add the pasta and stir a few times to ensure that the pasta does not stick to itself. Boil vigorously for the time recommended on the pasta package or until the pasta is tender.

While the pasta cooks, toss the roasted peppers, garlic, anchovies, olive oil, and lemon juice in a serving bowl.

Drain the pasta and toss it in the bowl with the sauce. Add the basil or parsley, cheese, salt, and pepper.

Smoky Corn and Rosemary Sauce

**Makes
4 servings**

Pasta traditionalists will look askance at this combination, but they are sure to be won over by its homey charm and unusual mixture of textures and flavors. The corn is juicy and sweet; the ham has smoke, a hint of salt, and a meaty chew; the rosemary lends a woodsy fragrance; and the tomato is all garden freshness. But the novel perfume of orange zest is what ties them all together, giving the whole the sweet scent of orange blossoms.

---

1 pound shaped pasta, such as wagon wheels or shells

2 tablespoons extra-virgin olive oil

1 cup diced ham

2 cups canned corn kernels, drained

1 tablespoon fresh rosemary leaves

Salt and freshly ground black pepper to taste

1 tablespoon minced orange zest

1 clove garlic, minced

2 cups diced tomatoes, canned or fresh

Bring a large pot of lightly salted water to a boil. Add the pasta and stir a few times to ensure that the pasta does not stick to itself. Boil vigorously for the time recommended on the pasta package or until the pasta is tender.

While the pasta cooks, heat the olive oil in a large skillet over medium-high heat, add the ham, and cook for 30 seconds. Add the corn and stir until heated through, about 1 minute. Add the rosemary, salt, pepper, orange zest, and garlic and stir to combine. Add the tomatoes and heat through. Adjust the seasoning with salt and pepper.

Drain the pasta and toss it with the sauce in a serving bowl.

Tuna, Hazelnut, and Garlic Sauce

**Makes
4 servings**

If you don't like canned tuna but you've tried only the water-packed kind, you owe yourself a portion of this pasta. The tuna is moist and full-flavored. The hazelnuts add a toasted richness that plays off a hefty dose of garlic and plenty of chopped fresh dill. Additional olive oil is added to help moisten the sauce. If you want to omit this oil, add about half a cup of the pasta water instead to keep the sauce from becoming too dry.

---

1 pound shaped pasta, such as shells

3 tablespoons extra-virgin olive oil

1 cup skinned hazelnuts, chopped

3 cloves garlic, minced

One 6-ounce can (approximately) tuna packed
 in oil

3 tablespoons chopped fresh dill

Salt and freshly ground black pepper to taste

Bring a large pot of lightly salted water to a boil. Add the pasta and stir a few times to ensure that the pasta does not stick to itself. Boil vigorously for the time recommended on the pasta package or until the pasta is tender.

While the pasta cooks, heat 1 tablespoon of the olive oil in a medium skillet over high heat until it is very hot, reduce the heat to low, add the hazelnuts, and stir until the nuts are lightly toasted, about 1 to 2 minutes. Remove from the heat and transfer to a serving bowl. Stir the garlic into the bowl. Add the tuna with its oil and break into small pieces with a fork. Stir in the remaining 2 tablespoons of oil, the dill, a little salt, and plenty of pepper.

Drain the pasta and toss it with the sauce in the bowl.

Marinated Artichoke and Feta Sauce

**Makes
4 servings**

Marinated artichoke hearts are a great convenience food. They maintain a firm consistency and a balance of flavors that vibrates between the pungency of the marinade and the natural sweetness of the vegetable. This sauce takes full advantage of those qualities, complementing the artichoke with a creamy liaison of feta cheese and plenty of fresh raw scallion.

1 pound curly pasta, such as fusilli or raddiatore

One 6-ounce jar marinated artichoke hearts, with liquid

4 ounces feta cheese, crumbled

2 tablespoons extra-virgin olive oil

4 scallions, trimmed of dark greens and roots and finely chopped

1/4 cup chopped fresh Italian (flat-leaf) parsley

2 tablespoons freshly grated Parmesan cheese

Salt and freshly ground black pepper to taste

Bring a large pot of lightly salted water to a boil. Add the pasta and stir a few times to ensure that the pasta does not stick to itself. Boil vigorously for the time recommended on the pasta package or until the pasta is tender.

While the pasta cooks, chop the artichoke hearts and combine them with their liquid, the feta, olive oil, scallions, and parsley in a serving bowl.

Drain the pasta, toss it in the bowl with the artichoke mixture, and add the Parmesan, salt, and pepper.

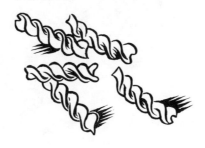

Roquefort, Walnut, and Fennel Sauce

**Makes
4 servings**

Here is a sauce that tastes as if it took hours to prepare. It's rich, slippery with cream and exotic flavors. The interplay of toasted walnuts, barely cooked fennel, and Roquefort cheese is at once surprising and sophisticated. Even blue-cheese cynics (of which I'm one) are bound to be won over.

1 pound curly or shaped pasta, such as
    fusilli or shells

2 tablespoons extra-virgin olive oil

$1/2$ cup walnuts, chopped

3 ribs fennel, peeled and thinly sliced

1 teaspoon dried thyme

6 ounces Roquefort cheese, crumbled

Salt and plenty of freshly ground black
    pepper to taste

Bring a large pot of lightly salted water to a boil. Add the pasta and stir a few times to ensure that the pasta does not stick to itself. Boil vigorously for the time recommended on the pasta package or until the pasta is tender.

While the pasta cooks, heat the olive oil in a medium skillet over medium-high heat, add the walnut pieces, and cook until they just begin to toast, about 1 minute. Add the fennel and thyme and continue cooking until the fennel is barely soft, about 3 minutes. Remove from the heat and stir in the cheese.

Drain the pasta and toss it with the sauce in a serving bowl. Season with salt and pepper.

Tomato, Basil, and Chèvre Sauce

**Makes
4 servings**

What could be simpler? A diced tomato, a cruet of oil, a bunch of basil, and fresh goat cheese. Chèvre, a French goat cheese, is widely available, its production having become a popular cottage industry in many communities. It is perfect for pasta. Creamy and slightly pungent, it pairs easily with most herbs and fresh vegetables. But more importantly, it melts on contact with hot noodles, forming a silken sauce in seconds.

1 pound pasta, any shape

2 large perfectly ripe tomatoes

¼ cup extra-virgin olive oil

24 basil leaves, chopped

4 ounces fresh chèvre, crumbled

2 cloves garlic, minced

Salt and freshly ground black pepper
  to taste

Bring a large pot of lightly salted water to a boil. Add the pasta and stir a few times to ensure that the pasta does not stick to itself. Boil vigorously for the time recommended on the pasta package or until the pasta is tender.

While the pasta cooks, remove and discard the stem ends from the tomatoes and chop the tomatoes into small dice. Toss the tomato in a serving bowl with the oil, basil, chèvre, garlic, salt, and plenty of pepper.

Drain the pasta and toss it in the bowl with the sauce.

Pumpkin Seed and Chili Pesto

**Makes
4 servings**

This sauce is an international hybrid. It's part pesto, part mole, and part salsa, and it's bursting with interesting flavors and textures. There's a kick of jalapeño, the aroma of oregano, and a bright burst of lime juice, but beyond all else, this is a sauce of pumpkin seeds. Make sure you buy the unsalted raw seeds called pepitas. *The best ones are long, thin, and dark green and are most commonly available in health-food stores. Pumpkin seeds have two-thirds less fat than other nuts.*

1 pound pasta, any shape

2 tablespoons vegetable oil

1/2 cup raw, hulled, unsalted pumpkin
  seeds (*pepitas*)

1 to 2 jalapeño peppers (depending on size),
  stemmed, seeded, and finely diced

1 poblano pepper, stemmed, seeded, and
  finely diced

1 teaspoon ground coriander

1 tablespoon chopped fresh oregano

Juice of 1 large lime

Salt and freshly ground black pepper to taste

1/4 cup extra-virgin olive oil

1/4 cup freshly grated Romano or
  Asiago cheese

Bring a large pot of lightly salted water to a boil. Add the pasta and stir a few times to ensure that the pasta does not stick to itself. Boil vigorously for the time recommended on the pasta package or until the pasta is tender.

While the pasta cooks, heat the oil in a medium skillet over medium-high heat, add the pumpkin seeds, jalapeño, and poblano, and cook until the pumpkin seeds pop vigorously, about 3 minutes. Transfer mixture to the bowl of a food processor and chop coarsely. Add the coriander, oregano, lime juice, salt, and pepper and process until finely chopped. With the processor running, add the oil and the cheese and process just until blended. Place the sauce in a serving bowl. Ladle a small amount of the pasta water into the pesto and stir to loosen.

When the pasta is ready, drain it and toss it with the sauce in the serving bowl.

Mushroom, Sweet Vinegar, and Garlic Sauce

**Makes
4 servings**

Mushrooms need to be tweaked. Meaty but bland, they beg for a dab of tomato, an infusion of herbs, or a scattering of cheese. In this recipe, the flavor boost comes from the reverberation of aged vinegar. Use either balsamic or sherry wine vinegar for their depth of flavor and their subtle blend of fruit, sugar, and acid.

1 pound shaped pasta, such as shells or ziti

1 small onion, chopped

1/4 cup olive oil

2 cloves garlic, minced

1 pound mushrooms, cleaned, stemmed, and chopped

1/2 cup dry white wine

1 teaspoon dried thyme

1 tablespoon tomato paste

Pinch of rubbed sage

Salt and freshly ground black pepper to taste

1 tablespoon balsamic or sherry wine vinegar

3 tablespoons chopped fresh Italian (flat-leaf) parsley

Freshly grated Parmesan cheese (optional)

Bring a large pot of lightly salted water to a boil. Add the pasta and stir a few times to ensure that the pasta does not stick to itself. Boil vigorously for the time recommended on the pasta package or until the pasta is tender.

While the pasta cooks, cook the onion in the olive oil in a large skillet over medium heat until softened, about 2 minutes. Add the garlic and mushrooms and cook until the mushrooms soften, about 3 more minutes. Add the wine, thyme, tomato paste, sage, salt, and pepper and cook 2 more minutes, stirring often. Add the vinegar and cook until slightly thickened, about 1 more minute. Stir in the parsley.

Drain the pasta and toss it with the sauce in a serving bowl. Serve with grated cheese if desired.

Peas and Prosciutto Sauce

**Makes
4 servings**

The combination of tiny baby peas and small shaped pasta is a classic. In texture, size, shape, and flavor, the fit is perfection. In this recipe, the sweetness of the peas is complemented by some salty prosciutto, bits of tart garden tomato, and an opulent splash of cream.

1 pound curly or shaped pasta, such as raddiatore or elbows

2 tablespoons olive oil

1 small onion, finely chopped

2 ounces prosciutto, diced

One 10-ounce box (about 2 cups) frozen baby peas

2 tablespoons finely chopped fresh mint

8 plum tomatoes, stemmed, seeded, and chopped (about 4 cups)

Salt and freshly ground black pepper to taste

$1/2$ cup heavy cream

Bring a large pot of lightly salted water to a boil. Add the pasta and stir a few times to ensure that the pasta does not stick to itself. Boil vigorously for the time recommended on the pasta package or until the pasta is tender.

While the pasta cooks, heat the oil in a medium skillet over medium heat, add the onion, and cook until softened, about 2 minutes. Add the prosciutto and the peas and cook for 2 minutes, until the peas are partially defrosted. Add the mint and the tomatoes and cook until the tomatoes are bubbling, about 4 minutes. Season with salt and pepper. Reduce the heat to low, stir in the cream, and remove from the heat.

Drain the pasta and toss it with the sauce in a serving bowl.

Chapter 4

Meat Sauces

Everyday Meat Sauce

Turkey Bolognese Sauce

Sausage and Mushroom Sauce

Chicken and Olive Sauce

Chilied Pork and Cilantro Sauce

Sausage in White Clam Sauce

Fennel Tomato-Beef Sauce

Chicken Livers in Sour Cream Sauce

Sicilian Meat Sauce

Chicken-Basil Sauce Thickened with White Beans

Like pure cream and aged cheese, meat in a pasta sauce is extravagant. Its plush texture and infusion of richness refashion pasta from a meal of sustenance to one of opulence. And it doesn't take much. Because just a few ounces of ground meat, sausage, chicken, or steak are enough to pump up a portion of sauce, a meat sauce can actually be an effective way to cut back on meat consumption.

There are several styles of meat sauce. The most typical is what Italian Philadelphia calls "red gravy"—a thick tomato sauce made denser with ground meat. It's slathered on lasagna noodles, ladled atop spaghetti, or used to gild a block of baked ziti, and it's the standard against which all other meat sauces are measured. Although there are as many recipes for red gravy as there are row homes in Italian South Philly, all of them are made pretty much the same way. Ground meat, usually beef, is browned with onion and garlic, tomatoes and herbs are added, and the whole is simmered until the sauce thickens enough to block an artery.

When you use chunks of meat, rather than the ubiquitous burger, a meat sauce takes on a completely different character. Without ground meat, the brothy part of the sauce becomes thinner and less integrated with the meat, making meat and sauce more like partners and less of a cohesive whole. In chunky meat sauces, the meat is more noticeable, swimming with bits of tomato and snipped herbs, and because it doesn't appear in every bite, its flavor often takes a back seat to the subtle tang of reduced wine or the smoke of a roasted pepper in the sauce.

By using bite-size pieces of tender meats, chunky sauces can be as quick and effortless as ground meat sauces. Small cubes of chicken or pork take only a few minutes to heat through, and then they're done. Because the sauce is not acquiring flavor or texture from the meat, there is nothing to be gained by prolonged cooking. In these sauces, consistency and flavor evolve spontaneously from the interchange of herbs, spices, and vegetables.

The third style of meat sauce is a variation on the chunky theme. The meat is counterbalanced by another equally assertive ingredient. The effect can be provocative, as it is when a rich, herby sausage is combined with saltwater clams. A sauce can be comforting when an old standard, such as liver and onions, finds new life saucing a plate of noodles, or it can play on a cacophony of flavors by juxtaposing chicken, tomato, and basil with a pungent array of olives.

I do not usually add cheese to meat sauces. Too often the result is unintentionally rich. Meat and cheese fulfill similar roles in a pasta sauce, creating complex flavors and opulent textures. In most cases, one is enough to do the job.

Everyday Meat Sauce

Makes 4 servings

There's nothing special about this sauce. Its flavor is straightforward, comes from readily available ingredients, and is appropriate with any shape pasta, so it will appeal to the pickiest eater in your family. Prepare it with your favorite ground meat and adjust the texture by using more or less of the diced tomato and tomato paste. Change the herbs and the seasonings according to what you have on hand, and it will turn into whatever sauce you want. Come to think of it, that is pretty special.

1 pound pasta, any shape
2 tablespoons olive oil
1 large onion, chopped
1 dried chili pepper (optional)
2 cloves garlic, minced
3/4 pound ground beef or turkey

4 cups diced tomatoes, canned or fresh, drained
2 tablespoons tomato paste
Salt and freshly ground black pepper to taste
1 tablespoon chopped fresh Italian (flat-leaf) parsley

Bring a large pot of lightly salted water to a boil. Add the pasta and stir a few times to ensure that the pasta does not stick to itself. Boil vigorously for the time recommended on the pasta package or until the pasta is tender.

While the pasta cooks, heat the oil in a large skillet over high heat, add the onion, and cook, stirring often, until browned, about 2 minutes. Add the chili pepper if desired, the garlic, and the meat and continue cooking until the meat loses its raw look. Add the tomatoes, tomato paste, salt, and pepper, bring to a boil, and simmer for 4 to 5 minutes. Adjust the salt and pepper and stir in the parsley. Remove the chili pepper.

Drain the pasta and toss it with the sauce in a serving bowl.

Turkey Bolognese Sauce

Recipes for Bolognese sauce are legion, each calling for a different permutation of the dairy-tomato-meat triumvirate that characterizes the signature dishes of Bologna. Unfortunately, most of these recipes also share hours of simmering. But not this one. By using precooked canned tomatoes, the sauce is thick before it begins, and since consistency is the principal reason for long, slow cooking of a tomato sauce, this shortcut saves hours of your time without sacrificing quality.

---

1 pound long pasta, such as fettuccine
  or linguine

2 tablespoons finely chopped onion

3 tablespoons olive oil

1 teaspoon dried basil

1/2 pound ground turkey

Salt and freshly ground black pepper
  to taste

3/4 cup milk

1/8 teaspoon ground nutmeg

3 cups crushed tomatoes in purée

Bring a large pot of lightly salted water to a boil. Add the pasta and stir a few times to ensure that the pasta does not stick to itself. Boil vigorously for the time recommended on the pasta package or until the pasta is tender.

While the pasta cooks, cook the onion in the oil in a large heavy skillet over medium-high heat until softened, about 2 minutes. Add the basil, turkey, salt, and pepper and stir until the meat loses its raw look, about 2 minutes. Add the milk and nutmeg and simmer until most of the liquid evaporates, about 3 minutes. Add the tomatoes, reduce the heat, and simmer until the pasta is ready, at least 10 minutes. Adjust seasoning.

Drain the pasta and toss it with the sauce in a serving bowl.

Sausage and Mushroom Sauce

**Makes
4 servings**

The flavor of this sauce is pure sausage, and its texture is all mushroom. When the sausage is finely chopped, its seasoning is dispersed throughout the sauce. You can either chop the sausage with a knife, or you can push the filling from its casing and cook it as you would any ground meat. When the cooking mushrooms release their liquid, they take on a meaty texture and their juices provide the fluid for the sauce, which is thickened and sweetened with a bit of tomato paste and a sprig of rosemary.

---

1 pound shaped pasta, such as penne or rotelle

1/2 pound mild Italian sausage, finely chopped

2 tablespoons olive oil

1/2 medium onion, chopped

1/4 pound mushrooms, cleaned, stemmed, and sliced

1 tablespoon fresh rosemary leaves

2 cloves garlic, minced

Large pinch of crushed red pepper flakes

2 tablespoons tomato paste

Salt and freshly ground black pepper to taste

Bring a large pot of lightly salted water to a boil. Add the pasta and stir a few times to ensure that the pasta does not stick to itself. Boil vigorously for the time recommended on the pasta package or until the pasta is tender.

While the pasta cooks, cook the sausage in a large nonstick skillet over medium-high heat until the meat loses its raw look, about 2 minutes, chopping and stirring as needed to help the sausage cook through evenly. Add the oil and the onion and continue cooking and stirring until the sausage begins to brown, about 3 more minutes. Add the mushrooms, rosemary, garlic, and red pepper flakes and cook until the mushrooms begin to release their liquid, about 2 more minutes. Add the tomato paste and 1/2 cup of the pasta cooking liquid and bring to a boil. Season with salt and pepper.

Drain the pasta and toss it with the sauce in a serving bowl.

Chicken and Olive Sauce

**Makes
4 servings**

The flavor of the Mediterranean is encapsulated in every olive. This sauce takes advantage of the musky richness of ripe black olives and the sharper tangy taste of unripe green olives for a multidimensional sauce that is fully flavored as soon as it is assembled.

1 pound shaped pasta, such as medium shells or orecchiette

2 tablespoons olive oil

1 large onion, chopped

1/2 pound boneless, skinless chicken breast, cut in 1-inch cubes

12 black olives (Niçoise, Kalamata, Mislinis), pitted and coarsely chopped

12 pitted green olives, coarsely chopped

1 cup diced tomatoes, fresh or canned

3 tablespoons chopped fresh basil

Salt and freshly ground black pepper to taste

Bring a large pot of lightly salted water to a boil. Add the pasta and stir a few times to ensure that the pasta does not stick to itself. Boil vigorously for the time recommended on the pasta package or until the pasta is tender.

While the pasta cooks, heat the oil in a large heavy skillet over medium-high heat, add the onion, and cook until softened, about 2 minutes. Add the chicken and cook until the chicken loses its raw look, about 2 minutes more. Add the olives, tomatoes, and basil and bring to a boil. Add 1 cup of the pasta cooking water and return to a boil. Season with salt and pepper.

Drain the pasta and toss with the sauce in a serving bowl.

Chilied Pork and Cilantro Sauce

**Makes
4 servings**

Pork has been revamped. Defatted and tenderized, the new pork needs only quick, brief cooking. More than that will dry and toughen it. This sauce does the job admirably. Bites of lean pork are stir-fried with chili, cumin, and coriander, simmered with tomato, and showered with cilantro. If you're not a fan of cilantro (also called fresh coriander), you can substitute basil, mint, Italian (flat-leaf) parsley, or chervil. With each one, you will create a different but equally effective flavor.

---

1 pound pasta, any shape

2 tablespoons olive oil

1 medium onion, chopped

1/2 pound boneless pork chop, cut in
   1-inch dice

3/4 teaspoon ground cumin

1/2 teaspoon ground coriander

1 teaspoon chili powder

1 clove garlic, minced

1 cup diced tomato, canned or fresh

3 tablespoons chopped fresh cilantro

Salt and freshly ground black pepper
   to taste

Bring a large pot of lightly salted water to a boil. Add the pasta and stir a few times to ensure that the pasta does not stick to itself. Boil vigorously for the time recommended on the pasta package or until the pasta is tender.

While the pasta cooks, heat the olive oil in a medium skillet over medium-high heat, add the onion, and cook until softened, about 2 minutes. Add the pork and cook until the meat loses its raw look, 1 to 2 minutes. Add the cumin, coriander, chili powder, and garlic and cook for 30 seconds. Add the tomato and cook for 1 minute more. Add the cilantro, salt, and pepper and simmer for 2 minutes.

Drain the pasta and toss it with the sauce in a serving bowl.

Sausage in White Clam Sauce

**Makes
4 servings**

The combination of sausage and seafood is a culinary tradition in Portugal and Spain. It's a natural: rich, meaty, cleanly salty. All that's needed is a bit of garlic and herb and a little sweet acid from some dry white wine. The sausage and clams deliver enough natural salinity that additional salt should not be necessary.

---

24 littleneck clams

1 pound shaped pasta, such as medium shells or penne

6 ounces mild Italian sausage, cut in small slices

1/4 cup olive oil

1 medium onion, chopped

1 clove garlic, minced

1/2 teaspoon dried thyme

1 cup dry white wine

2 tablespoons chopped fresh Italian (flat-leaf) parsley

Pinch of crushed red pepper flakes

Place the clams in a large bowl, cover with cold water, swirl in the water to remove surface dirt, drain, and cover again with fresh water.

Bring a large pot of lightly salted water to a boil. Add the pasta and stir a few times to ensure that the pasta does not stick to itself. Boil vigorously for the time recommended on the pasta package or until the pasta is tender.

While the pasta cooks, cook the sausage in a heavy skillet over medium-high heat until the meat loses its raw look, about 1 minute. Add the oil and the onion and cook until the onion is softened, about 2 minutes. Add the garlic, thyme, and wine and bring the mixture to a rolling boil. Drain the clams and add them to the skillet. Add the parsley and pepper flakes. Cover the pan and cook until the clams open, about 4 minutes.

Drain the pasta and toss it with the sauce in a serving bowl.

Fennel Tomato-Beef Sauce

**Makes
4 servings**

This is a straightforward tomato-and-beef sauce, but with one aromatic exception. It has been invaded by fennel. The sauce starts with fresh fennel and later ups the ante with a bit of ground fennel seed. The finished sauce glows with a licorice flavor that blends seamlessly with tomato. Most markets sell fresh fennel year round. It is sometimes sold as fresh anise.

---

1 pound pasta, any shape

2 tablespoons olive oil

³/₄ pound ground beef or turkey

1 medium onion, chopped

2 teaspoons fennel seed, ground

3 ribs fresh fennel, cut in medium dice

1 clove garlic, minced

1¹/₂ cups canned crushed tomatoes

1 cup diced tomatoes (or additional canned crushed tomatoes)

Salt and freshly ground black pepper to taste

Bring a large pot of lightly salted water to a boil. Add the pasta and stir a few times to ensure that the pasta does not stick to itself. Boil vigorously for the time recommended on the pasta package or until the pasta is tender.

While the pasta cooks, heat the oil in a large heavy skillet over medium-high heat. Add the meat and cook until it loses its raw look, about 1 minute, stirring often. Add the onion, ground fennel, and fresh fennel and cook another 2 minutes, stirring often. Add the garlic, tomatoes, and 1 cup of the pasta cooking water. Simmer for 3 minutes. Season with salt and pepper.

Transfer the sauce to a pasta serving bowl. Drain the pasta and toss it with the sauce in the bowl.

Chicken Livers in Sour Cream Sauce

**Makes
4 servings**

In Slavic cooking, the combination of sautéed chicken livers, onions, and sour cream is a pasta sauce. Traditionally, the ingredients are simmered together and served over broad egg noodles, so the switch to Italian pasta is natural. The secret to success is cooking the livers quickly—and stopping before they cook through. Test by touching. As soon as the fattest liver in the pan feels firm, the sauce is done. Sour cream is added off the heat. Reduced-fat sour cream or yogurt can be substituted for regular sour cream.

---

1 pound shaped pasta, such as medium shells or wagon wheels

2 leeks (white part only), root ends removed

3/4 pound chicken livers

2 tablespoons vegetable oil

3 tablespoons chopped fresh dill

3/4 cup dry white wine

Salt and freshly ground black pepper to taste

1 cup sour cream, regular or reduced-fat

Bring a large pot of lightly salted water to a boil. Add the pasta and stir a few times to ensure that the pasta does not stick to itself. Boil vigorously for the time recommended on the pasta package or until the pasta is tender.

While the pasta cooks, cut the leeks in half lengthwise, run under cold water to rid them of dirt and sand, chop finely, and set aside. Cut the chicken livers into lobes, trimming away any fat and gristle, and cut into large pieces. Heat the oil in a large skillet over high heat, add the leeks, and cook for 1 minute, stirring often. Add the chicken livers, cooking and stirring until they have lost their raw look, about 1 minute. Add the dill and wine and simmer for 3 minutes or until reduced by half. Season with salt and pepper.

Drain the pasta and toss it with the liver mixture and the sour cream in a serving bowl.

Sicilian Meat Sauce

**Makes
4 servings**

The combination of mint and meat enters into the Italian tradition from the Middle East through Sicily. The herb's sweet, mentholated coolness lightens the sauce, as does the use of blended ground meat. Meat loaf mix is a widely sold combination of veal, pork, and beef that's milder, moister, and softer than ground beef alone.

---

1 pound pasta, any shape

1 tablespoon olive oil

1/2 pound meat loaf mix (see note above)

1 medium onion, chopped

1 clove garlic, minced

1/2 cup chopped fresh mint (about 1 bunch)

1/8 teaspoon dried oregano

Pinch of crushed red pepper flakes

2 cups tomato purée

1/2 teaspoon sugar

Salt and freshly ground black pepper to taste

Bring a large pot of lightly salted water to a boil. Add the pasta and stir a few times to ensure that the pasta does not stick to itself. Boil vigorously for the time recommended on the pasta package or until the pasta is tender.

While the pasta cooks, heat the oil in a large heavy skillet over medium-high heat. Add the meat loaf mixture and cook, chopping and stirring to help it cook evenly, until the meat loses its raw look, about 2 minutes. Add the onion and continue cooking and stirring until the meat begins to brown, about 3 more minutes. Add the garlic, mint, oregano, red pepper flakes, tomato purée, and sugar and simmer for 2 minutes. Season with salt and pepper.

Drain the pasta and toss it with the sauce in a serving bowl.

Chicken-Basil Sauce Thickened with White Beans

Makes 4 servings

This classically flavored white-wine sauce, enriched with chicken, uses a novel thickener—puréed white beans.

---

1 pound shaped pasta, such as medium shells, penne, or ziti

1/4 cup extra-virgin olive oil

1/2 pound boneless, skinless chicken breast, cut in 1-inch dice

2 cloves garlic, minced

1 cup dry white wine

1/2 cup chopped fresh basil

1 cup cooked white beans, home-cooked or canned, drained

Salt and freshly ground black pepper to taste

Bring a large pot of lightly salted water to a boil. Add the pasta and stir a few times to ensure that the pasta does not stick to itself. Boil vigorously for the time recommended on the pasta package or until the pasta is tender.

While the pasta cooks, heat the oil in a large heavy skillet over medium-high heat, add the chicken, and cook until it loses its raw look, about 2 minutes. Add the garlic and white wine and boil for 3 minutes. Add the basil and the beans and return the mixture to a boil. With the back of a large fork or spoon, mash about half the beans. Season with salt and pepper and thin the sauce, if necessary, with a little of the pasta water.

Drain the pasta and toss it with the sauce in a serving bowl.

Chapter 5

Seafood Sauces

Crab, Tarragon, and Cream Sauce

Hot Pepper Clam Sauce

Mussels Rosa

Shrimp, Asparagus, and Dill Sauce

Salmon, Capers, and Rosemary Sauce

Orange Roughy, Tomato, and Orange Sauce

Crab, Herb Cheese, and Spinach Sauce

Sun-Dried Tomato and Calamari Sauce

Sardine and Olive Sauce

Lemon Scallop Sauce

T he trick to cooking seafood is knowing when to stop. Compared to other meats, the muscle fiber of fish is weak, which makes it quick and easy to cook but just as easy to overcook. For a pasta sauce, this means the fish is always the *last* ingredient to go in; when it's done, so is the sauce.

If the fish is cut in chunks, as it is for most sauces, it will cook through especially fast. Stir carefully so as not to break the pieces unnecessarily, and remove the pan from the heat as soon as you see the first signs of flaking. For best results, the flakes should still look moist in the center when you remove the sauce from the heat.

Shellfish, too, are highly sensitive to heat. Sauces with clams or mussels are done as soon the shellfish pop open. Any more cooking will start to toughen the fish and turn the meat hard and rubbery.

For pasta sauce, clams and mussels are steamed right in the sauce. They need only a few inches of simmering liquid in the bottom of a large pot. When the shells open, the clams and mussels will release their own juices into the sauce, giving it flavor and increasing its volume. ·

Before steaming, clams and mussels should be scrubbed with clean cold water and a stiff brush to remove any barnacles and surface dirt. Then it is a good idea to soak them for a while in some clear running water to give them a chance to purge themselves of any sand that might be inside their shells.

Shrimp are easier to clean. Often they are sold shelled and cleaned, but even if they're not, the shell peels off easily and cleaning involves the simple step of slitting the shrimp down its back and washing out the dark vein that lies just under the skin.

Large-size shrimp are best for pasta sauce. Extra-large, jumbo, colossal, and whatever other giganticized names fish purveyors come up with are going to cost a lot more, and since they must be cut to bite size anyway, the added expense is not worth it. Look for shrimp with a 26–30 count. The count is the approximate number of shrimp per pound, in this case about seven per serving. They will be a generous bite size, and they will heat through quickly. Shrimp are done cooking as soon as they lose their raw look and become firm. Usually this takes a minute or less.

Crabmeat is even easier to clean and cook than shrimp. Do not hassle with live crabs for quick-cooking pasta sauces. Shelled crabmeat is precooked, so it needs only to be warmed, and it comes in a number of sizes. Lump crabmeat is the best for sauce. It has a mixture of impressive large chunks interspersed with smaller pieces that will integrate with the sauce. Do not bother with jumbo lump crab, which has bigger pieces and is much more expensive. Do, however, spend the extra money for fresh crabmeat rather than canned, pasteurized products. The heat of pasteurization overcooks crab, making it tough and dry.

Crab, Tarragon, and Cream Sauce

Makes 4 servings

I am not a great fan of tarragon. I frequently find its sweetness and floral fragrance overpowering. But I think it's great with crab. The combination of herbal sweetness and ocean saltiness is a winner. Be careful to not use too much. If you want to substitute dried tarragon for fresh, reduce the amount to ½ teaspoon.

1 pound pasta, any shape

2 tablespoons butter

¼ cup finely chopped shallots

1 teaspoon chopped fresh tarragon

½ cup dry white wine

1 cup fish broth or 1 cup water and ½ fish bouillon cube (see note)

2 tablespoons chopped fresh Italian (flat-leaf) parsley

6 ounces lump crabmeat, pieces of shell removed

1 cup light cream

Pinch of cayenne pepper

Salt and freshly ground black pepper to taste

Bring a large pot of lightly salted water to a boil. Add the pasta and stir a few times to ensure that the pasta does not stick to itself. Boil vigorously for the time recommended on the pasta package or until the pasta is tender.

While the pasta cooks, melt the butter in a medium skillet over medium heat, add the shallots and tarragon, and cook until the shallots soften, about 2 minutes. Add the wine, raise the heat to high, and boil for 1 minute. Add the fish broth and boil until the liquid reduces to about ⅓ cup. Add the parsley, crabmeat, and cream, bring to a simmer, and simmer until slightly thickened, about 1 minute. Season with cayenne, salt, and pepper.

Drain the pasta and toss it with the sauce in a serving bowl.

Note: *Knorr produces a high-quality fish bouillon cube that is available nationwide.*

Hot Pepper Clam Sauce

**Makes
4 servings**

This southwestern version of clam sauce has the requisite bits of jalapeño, tomato, and cilantro that one would expect, but the real stars are the clams. There are a lot of them, and it is their flavor, texture, and natural juices that create the bulk of this sauce. Use littleneck clams, the smaller the better, and don't overcook them or they will turn rubbery and fishy tasting. Because clams are salty, you probably won't need additional salt, so taste before serving.

---

4 dozen littleneck clams

1 pound shaped pasta, such as large shells or raddiatore

1/4 cup olive oil

1 medium onion, chopped

2 large jalapeño peppers, stemmed, seeded, and minced

2 cloves garlic, minced

2 teaspoons ground coriander

2 cups diced tomatoes, fresh or canned

3 tablespoons chopped fresh cilantro

Freshly ground black pepper to taste

Place the clams in a large bowl, cover with cold water, swirl in the water to remove surface dirt, drain, and cover again with fresh water. Set aside.

Bring a large pot of lightly salted water to a boil. Add the pasta and stir a few times to ensure that the pasta does not stick to itself. Boil vigorously for the time recommended on the pasta package or until the pasta is tender.

While the pasta cooks, heat the olive oil in a large deep skillet over medium-high heat, add the onion and jalapeño, and cook until the onion softens, about 2 minutes. Add the garlic and coriander and stir. Add the tomatoes and bring to a boil. Drain the clams and add them to the skillet, add the cilantro and a little black pepper, cover the pan, and cook until the clams have opened, about 4 minutes.

Drain the pasta and toss it with the sauce in a serving bowl.

Mussels Rosa

This is a lighter, muted version of the classic mussels in red sauce. Instead of using a thick purée, this sauce stays discreetly in the background. It is translucent, tinged with lemon, and permeated with basil.

---

2 pounds mussels, cleaned

1 pound shaped pasta, such as large
   shells or bowties

2 tablespoons olive oil

1/2 medium onion, chopped

2 cloves garlic, minced

Pinch of crushed red pepper flakes

2 cups canned crushed tomatoes

Julienned zest of 1 medium lemon

1/4 cup chopped fresh basil

Salt and freshly ground black pepper to taste

Discard any open mussels that won't close. Place the remaining mussels in a large bowl, cover with cold water, swirl in the water to remove surface dirt, drain, and cover again with fresh water.

Bring a large pot of lightly salted water to a boil. Add the pasta and stir a few times to ensure that the pasta does not stick to itself. Boil vigorously for the time recommended on the pasta package or until the pasta is tender.

While the pasta cooks, heat the olive oil in a large heavy-bottomed saucepan over medium-high heat, add the onion, and cook until softened, about 2 minutes. Add the garlic and red pepper flakes and stir. Add half the crushed tomatoes and the lemon zest and bring to a boil.

Drain the mussels and add them to the pan. Add the basil, salt, and pepper, cover the pan, and cook until all the mussels have opened, about 3 minutes, shaking the pan every minute.

Drain the pasta and toss it in a serving bowl with the mussels, the sauce, the remaining crushed tomatoes, and additional salt and pepper if needed.

Shrimp, Asparagus, and Dill Sauce

**Makes
4 servings**

I am a sucker for asparagus and pink seafood—salmon, shrimp, charr, cray-fish. I love the dramatic color combination, the subtle shifts in texture, and the juxtaposition of sweet fish and slightly acrid asparagus. What's more, the two cook at very similar rates, so timing is a snap.

---

1 pound tube-shaped pasta, such
    as ziti or penne

1 tablespoon vegetable oil

1 tablespoon butter

2 medium shallots, finely chopped

1/2 pound asparagus, trimmed and cut in
    2-inch lengths

1 clove garlic, minced

1/4 cup chopped fresh dill

1 pound medium shrimp (31–35 count),
    peeled and deveined

1/4 cup extra-virgin olive oil

Salt and freshly ground black pepper to taste

Bring a large pot of lightly salted water to a boil. Add the pasta and stir a few times to ensure that the pasta does not stick to itself. Boil vigorously for the time recommended on the pasta package or until the pasta is tender.

While the pasta cooks, heat the vegetable oil and butter in a medium skillet over medium heat until the butter melts, add the shallots, and cook until softened, about 2 minutes. Add the asparagus and cook until it loses its raw look, about 2 minutes. Add 1 cup of the pasta water, raise the heat to medium-high, and boil until the asparagus turn bright green, about 2 minutes. Add the garlic, dill, and shrimp and stir to combine. Remove from the heat and stir in the olive oil, salt, and pepper.

Drain the pasta and toss it in a serving bowl with the sauce, adding more salt and pepper if needed.

Salmon, Capers, and Rosemary Sauce

**Makes
4 servings**

Capers flirt with salmon, playing off the fish's rich flavor and moisture with bright sparks of brine and a toothsome chew. The trick to this sauce is in cooking the salmon. Don't overdo it. As soon as the salmon starts to flake, while it is still moist in the center, stop cooking. Its residual heat will continue steaming the fish.

---

1 pound shaped pasta, such as elbows,
   shells, or raddiatore

1/4 cup olive oil

1 medium onion, chopped

2 cloves garlic, minced

1 tablespoon fresh rosemary leaves

2 tablespoons capers

1/2 cup dry white wine

1/2 pound salmon fillets, skinned, boned, and
   cut in 4 pieces

Salt and freshly ground black pepper to taste

Bring a large pot of lightly salted water to a boil. Add the pasta and stir a few times to ensure that the pasta does not stick to itself. Boil vigorously for the time recommended on the pasta package or until the pasta is tender.

While the pasta cooks, heat the oil in a heavy skillet over medium-high heat, add the onion, and cook until softened, about 2 minutes. Add the garlic, rosemary, and capers and cook 30 seconds more. Add the wine, bring to a rolling boil, add the salmon, and cook until the fish breaks into moist flakes, about 2 minutes. Do not cook until dry. Season with salt and pepper.

Drain the pasta and toss it with the sauce in a serving bowl, seasoning with additional salt and pepper if needed.

Orange Roughy, Tomato, and Orange Sauce

**Makes
4 servings**

This sauce can be made with any firm white-fleshed fish, such as red snapper or flounder. Its flavor comes from the intoxicating combination of tomatoes, orange, and basil. You can use a zester or a fine grater to remove the zest from the orange, but make sure the fruit itself is very firm. Any softness will cause the peel to split while the zest is being removed.

---

1 pound shaped pasta, such as shells, elbows, or penne

2 tablespoons olive oil

1 large onion, chopped

2 cloves garlic, minced

Grated zest and juice of 1 firm orange

2 cups diced tomatoes, fresh or canned

2 tablespoons chopped fresh basil

1/2 pound firm white fish fillets (such as orange roughy, St. Peter's fish, or catfish), cut in 1-inch dice

Salt and freshly ground black pepper to taste

Bring a large pot of lightly salted water to a boil. Add the pasta and stir a few times to ensure that the pasta does not stick to itself. Boil vigorously for the time recommended on the pasta package or until the pasta is tender.

While the pasta cooks, heat the oil in a medium skillet over medium-high heat, add the onion, and cook until softened, about 2 minutes. Add the garlic, orange zest, and tomatoes and heat to a simmer. Add the basil and fish and simmer until the fish breaks into moist flakes, about 1 to 2 minutes. Do not overcook. Add the orange juice, salt, and pepper.

Drain the pasta and toss it with the sauce in a serving bowl, seasoning with additional salt and pepper if needed.

Crab, Herb Cheese, and Spinach Sauce

**Makes
4 servings**

Packaged herb cream cheese gives this pasta sauce instant flavor and a creamy consistency. Alone, the cheese would be too dense, but by cooking it with spinach, the juices from the vegetable moisten the cream cheese, lending it just the right amount of fluid to melt into a perfect sauce.

---

1 pound shaped pasta, such as medium
  shells or penne

2 tablespoons olive oil

1 medium onion, chopped

1 clove garlic, minced

One 10-ounce bag fresh spinach, stemmed
  and washed (but not dried)

3 ounces herb-and-garlic cream cheese

6 ounces lump crabmeat, pieces of shell
  removed

Salt and freshly ground black pepper to taste

Bring a large pot of lightly salted water to a boil. Add the pasta and stir a few times to ensure that the pasta does not stick to itself. Boil vigorously for the time recommended on the pasta package or until the pasta is tender.

While the pasta cooks, heat the olive oil in a medium skillet over medium-high heat, add the onion, and cook until softened, about 2 minutes. Add the garlic and the spinach, cover the pan, and cook until the spinach has wilted, about 1 to 2 minutes. Add the cream cheese and stir until it melts. Add the crabmeat, salt, and pepper and heat through.

Drain the pasta and toss it with the sauce in a serving bowl, adding more salt and pepper if needed.

Sun-Dried Tomato and Calamari Sauce

**Makes
4 servings**

Calamari (the appetizing name for squid) are much easier to appreciate on the plate than in the imagination. Calamari are very clean and subtle tasting. They are the least "fishy" of all seafood, and if you buy them already cleaned, they are effortless to prepare. Each piece has two sections. Slice the sack-like body into rings and cut the tentacles and legs in half. Calamari do not need a lot of cooking, which makes them the perfect ingredient for a quick sauce. (Simmer too long, in fact, and they will turn into little rubber bands.)

1 pound shaped pasta, such as shells
   or penne

2 tablespoons extra-virgin olive oil

1 pound cleaned calamari, bodies sliced in
   rings, tentacles and legs cut in half

14 sun-dried tomatoes packed in olive oil,
   finely chopped

2 cloves garlic, finely chopped

3 tablespoons chopped fresh basil

2 tablespoons oil from sun-dried tomatoes

Salt and freshly ground black pepper to taste

Bring a large pot of lightly salted water to a boil. Add the pasta and stir a few times to ensure that the pasta does not stick to itself. Boil vigorously for the time recommended on the pasta package or until the pasta is tender.

While the pasta cooks, heat the olive oil in a medium skillet over high heat, add the calamari, and toss until they lose their raw look, about 30 seconds. Reduce the heat to medium and add the sun-dried tomatoes, garlic, and basil. Continue cooking until the calamari are firm, about 1 to 2 minutes more. Stir in the oil from the tomatoes and season with salt and pepper.

Drain the pasta and toss it with the sauce in a serving bowl, adding more salt and pepper if needed.

Sardine and Olive Sauce

**Makes
4 servings**

Relax. If the thought of a sardine sauce makes you balk, there are 99 other sauces in this book. I can only encourage you to put aside your prejudice and dive in. This sauce is delicious—rich, pungent, and full of flavor. Except for cooking the pasta, you don't even have to turn on the stove.

---

1 pound pasta, any shape

⅓ cup imported black olives (such as Kalamata, Mislinis, or Niçoise), pitted and coarsely chopped

One 3¾-ounce tin sardines packed in olive oil

2 cloves garlic, minced

Pinch of crushed red pepper flakes

¼ cup extra-virgin olive oil

Salt and freshly ground black pepper to taste

¼ cup chopped fresh Italian (flat-leaf) parsley

Bring a large pot of lightly salted water to a boil. Add the pasta and stir a few times to ensure that the pasta does not stick to itself. Boil vigorously for the time recommended on the pasta package or until the pasta is tender.

While the pasta cooks, combine the olives, sardines, garlic, red pepper flakes, olive oil, salt, pepper, and parsley in a serving bowl until the sardines have broken in pieces.

Drain the pasta and toss it with the sauce in the serving bowl, adding more salt and pepper if needed.

Lemon Scallop Sauce

**Makes
4 servings**

This delicate sauce is pale gold, flecked with bits of red and green. Do not cook it too long. The butter burns easily, and the scallops can quickly dry out. Keep the heat medium to low and you'll be fine. As soon as the scallops heat through, the sauce is ready.

---

1 pound pasta, any shape

6 tablespoons butter

1 pound sea scallops, sliced horizontally

3 cloves garlic, minced

Pinch of crushed red pepper flakes

Juice of 1 large lemon

Salt and freshly ground black pepper to taste

2 tablespoons chopped fresh dill

Bring a large pot of lightly salted water to a boil. Add the pasta and stir a few times to ensure that the pasta does not stick to itself. Boil vigorously for the time recommended on the pasta package or until the pasta is tender.

While the pasta cooks, heat half the butter in a medium skillet over medium heat, add the scallops, and toss until they lose their raw look, about 1 minute. Add the garlic, red pepper flakes, lemon juice, salt, and pepper. Bring to a simmer and stir in the dill. Remove from the heat and stir in the remaining butter.

Drain the pasta and toss it with the sauce in a serving bowl, adding more salt and pepper if needed.

Chapter 6

Vegetable Sauces

Broccoli, Garlic, and Cheese Sauce

Winter Squash, Pine Nuts, and Cheese Sauce

Lemon Garlic Green Bean Sauce

Wild Mushroom Persillade

Broccoli Rabe and Potato Sauce With Lotsa Garlic

Three-Mushroom Sauce

Baby Peas, Tomato, and Cream Sauce

Pecorino Spinach Sauce

Three-Pepper Sauce

Summer Squash and Pepper Cheese Sauce

A bumper crop of broccoli or a fortuitous finding of wild mushrooms has always been reason enough to put on a pot of pasta. Some vegetables, tossed simply with cheese and a garnish of herbs, are all you need to turn noodles into a meal.

And here's a bonus: Vegetables that need to be boiled can be cooked right along with the pasta. Blanch broccoli or asparagus in the pasta water a few minutes before the noodles are ready, and add longer-cooking potatoes along with the pasta. Delicate leaves, like spinach, can either be sautéed with the other sauce ingredients or wilted in the pasta water just as the pasta finishes boiling.

When vegetables are cooked and drained with the pasta, a finished sauce needs nothing more than a quick sauté of onion and garlic or a gilding of oil and cheese. Coat ziti and asparagus in a creamy Alfredo sauce that's assembled right in the serving bowl. Toss ruffled raddiatore and spinach with Pecorino Romano cheese and some garlic. Green beans boiled with penne need just a bit of lemon zest, crushed pepper, and garlic.

Delicate vegetables like tomatoes, zucchini, and peppers are better cooked quickly in a separate pan. (Boiling them with the pasta would waterlog these vegetables in seconds.) Just sauté them in a thin film of olive oil while the pasta cooks. Most vegetables will release enough liquid during cooking to create a sauce on their own, but a ladle of pasta water can be added to the sauté pan if the mixture becomes too dry.

Don't be afraid to enrich vegetable sauces by adding flavorful oils and cheese. All vegetables, except olives and avocados, are very low in fat. Their flavors are usually subtle, and even when a vegetable sauce seems packed with flavor in the pan, it can turn instantly bland once it is combined with plain pasta. The small amount of fat from a strategic glaze of olive oil or a dusting of grated cheese will help bolster all the other flavors in the sauce.

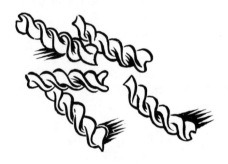

Broccoli, Garlic, and Cheese Sauce

**Makes
4 servings**

Broccoli florets are added to the cooking pasta minutes before it's done so that both emerge perfectly al dente. After that, all that's needed is a hint of garlic, a splash of fruity olive oil, and a handful of freshly grated cheese.

1 pound shaped pasta, such as ziti or
    raddiatore

1 bunch broccoli (about 1 pound),
    cut into florets

1 clove garlic, minced

3 tablespoons extra-virgin olive oil

1/2 cup freshly grated Parmesan and/or
    Romano cheese

Salt and freshly ground black pepper to taste

Bring a large pot of lightly salted water to a boil. Add the pasta and stir a few times to ensure that the pasta does not stick to itself. Boil vigorously for the time recommended on the pasta package or until the pasta is tender. Four minutes before the pasta will finish cooking, add the broccoli to the water.

While the pasta cooks, combine the garlic, olive oil, cheese, salt, and pepper in a serving bowl.

Drain the pasta and broccoli and toss with the garlic mixture.

Winter Squash, Pine Nuts, and Cheese Sauce

**Makes
4 servings**

The festive pumpkin-stuffed tortellis and raviolis of Modena are the inspiration for this unusual pasta sauce. Shreds of sweet winter squash are cooked with the pasta, providing a lightly crunchy counterpoint to the toasted pine nuts and pungent cheese that complete the sauce.

---

1 pound tube-shaped pasta, such as ziti
   or penne

1 pound acorn or butternut squash, peeled,
   seeded, and shredded

1/2 cup pine nuts

1/4 cup extra-virgin olive oil

1 1/2 cloves garlic, minced

3/4 cup freshly grated Parmesan or Romano
   cheese

Salt and freshly ground black pepper to taste

Bring a large pot of lightly salted water to a boil. Add the pasta and stir a few times to ensure that the pasta does not stick to itself. Boil vigorously for the time recommended on the pasta package or until the pasta is tender. Five minutes before the pasta will finish cooking, add the squash and stir briefly.

While the pasta cooks, toast the pine nuts in a hot dry skillet, in a toaster oven at 400°F, or in a microwave oven for 3 to 4 minutes at full power.

Drain the pasta and squash and toss them with the olive oil, garlic, cheese, salt, pepper, and pine nuts in a serving bowl.

Lemon Garlic Green Bean Sauce

**Makes
4 servings**

Fresh green beans echo the shape and texture of pencil-thin ziti or quills of penne. The two are tossed with a fragrant mixture of garlic and lemon that's subtle enough to let the delicate flavor of the beans shine through but novel enough to give the dish a distinct citrusy profile.

1 pound tube-shaped pasta, such
   as ziti or penne
1 pound green beans, trimmed
3 tablespoons olive oil
1 medium onion, chopped

Pinch of crushed red pepper flakes
3 cloves garlic, minced
Finely grated zest of 1 lemon

Bring a large pot of lightly salted water to a boil. Add the pasta and stir a few times to ensure that the pasta does not stick to itself. Boil vigorously for the time recommended on the pasta package or until the pasta is tender. Three minutes before the pasta will finish cooking, add the green beans to the pot.

While the pasta cooks, heat the olive oil in a large skillet over medium-high heat, add the onion, and cook until softened, about 2 minutes. Add the red pepper flakes and the garlic and cook for 30 seconds. Remove from the heat and stir in the lemon zest.

Drain the pasta and green beans and toss them with the sauce in a serving bowl.

Wild Mushroom Persillade

**Makes
4 servings**

Cepes, shiitakes, crimini, morels—any or all of the wild mushrooms commonly available at your local market will be glorified by this elegantly simple sauce. The mushrooms are sautéed, scented with wine and garlic, tinged by bits of tomato, and showered with an avalanche of parsley (hence the recipe name). But mostly the rich flavor of the mushrooms themselves star in this sauce, making it hearty enough for midwinter feasting and plush enough for a sophisticated dinner party.

---

1 pound pasta, any kind

3 tablespoons extra-virgin olive oil

1 medium onion, chopped

8 ounces wild mushrooms, any kind, cleaned, stemmed, and sliced

8 ounces white mushrooms, cleaned, stemmed, and sliced

1 cup dry white wine

2 cloves garlic, minced

1 tomato, diced

1/2 cup chopped fresh Italian (flat-leaf) parsley

Salt and freshly ground black pepper to taste

Bring a large pot of lightly salted water to a boil. Add the pasta, and stir a few times to ensure that the pasta does not stick to itself. Boil vigorously for the time recommended on the pasta package or until the pasta is tender.

While the pasta cooks, heat the olive oil in a large nonstick skillet over medium-high heat, add the onion, and cook until softened, about 2 minutes. Add the mushrooms and cook until softened, about 3 minutes. Add the wine, bring to a boil, and boil for 2 minutes. Add the garlic and tomato and heat through. Stir in the parsley, salt, and pepper.

Drain the pasta and toss with the sauce in a serving bowl.

Broccoli Rabe and Potato Sauce with Lotsa Garlic

**Makes
4 servings**

Broccoli rabe, the nonheading form of broccoli, is beloved and hated in equal measure. If you appreciate the bitter edge of endive and radicchio, you'll probably adore broccoli rabe, but it might take a few tastes to become acclimated. In this recipe, it is set off by a hefty dose of garlic and a balm of boiled potatoes, which both tame the rabe and melt into a creamy sauce that coats the pasta.

1 pound shaped pasta, such as penne
  or raddiatore

1 to 1¼ pounds white potatoes,
  cut in 1-inch dice

¼ cup extra-virgin olive oil

1 medium onion, chopped

1 bunch broccoli rabe, ends trimmed,
  cut in 1½-inch pieces, washed, and left wet

Pinch of crushed red pepper flakes

3 cloves garlic, minced

Salt and freshly ground black pepper to taste

⅓ cup freshly grated Parmesan or Romano
  cheese

Bring a large pot of lightly salted water to a boil. Add the pasta and the potatoes and stir a few times to ensure that the pasta does not stick to itself. Boil vigorously for the time recommended on the pasta package or until the pasta is tender.

While the pasta cooks, heat the olive oil over medium-high heat in a large skillet, add the onion, and cook for 1 minute. Add the wet broccoli rabe, cover, and cook until it has wilted, about 3 minutes. Add the red pepper flakes, cover, and cook for 2 minutes more. Remove from the heat and stir in the garlic, salt, and pepper.

Drain the pasta and potatoes and toss them with the sauce and the cheese in a serving bowl.

Three-Mushroom Sauce

**Makes
4 servings** *Dried wild mushrooms give this sauce its depth of flavor and mahogany hue. The first step is rehydration. Soaking softens and plumps the mushrooms and yields a richly flavored cooking liquid. Before using the soaking liquid, be sure that any dirty sediment from the mushrooms is removed, either by straining through a coffee filter or paper towel or by carefully pouring off the clear liquid and leaving the sediment behind.*

---

¹/₃ ounce dried wild mushrooms,
   any variety

1¹/₂ cups boiling water

1 pound shaped pasta, such as shells
   or orecchiette

2 tablespoons extra-virgin olive oil

1 medium onion, chopped

7 ounces fresh shiitake mushrooms, cleaned,
   stemmed, and sliced

7 ounces white mushrooms, cleaned,
   stemmed, and sliced

2 cloves garlic, minced

2 tablespoons tomato paste

¹/₄ cup chopped fresh Italian (flat-leaf) parsley

Salt and freshly ground black pepper to taste

Place the dried wild mushrooms in the boiling water to soak for about 10 minutes.

Bring a large pot of lightly salted water to a boil. Add the pasta and stir a few times to ensure that the pasta does not stick to itself. Boil vigorously for the time recommended on the pasta package or until the pasta is tender.

While the pasta cooks, remove the mushrooms from the soaking liquid and squeeze the excess liquid from the mushrooms back into the bowl. Slice the mushrooms and strain the soaking liquid through a coffee filter or a paper towel to remove the sediment. Reserve the soaking liquid.

Heat the olive oil in a large skillet over medium-high heat, add the onion, and cook until softened, about 2 minutes. Add the soaked wild mushrooms, the fresh shiitakes, and the white mushrooms and cook for 2 minutes, stirring often. Add the garlic, mushroom soaking liquid, and tomato paste and cook until the liquid reduces by half, about 3 to 4 minutes. Add the parsley, salt, and pepper and stir.

Drain the pasta and toss with the mushroom sauce in a serving bowl.

Baby Peas, Tomato, and Cream Sauce

**Makes
4 servings**

The appearance of tiny baby peas in the early spring would be reason enough to prepare this pasta, even if it did not have so much else going for it. The dish is beautiful, with hundreds of emerald pearls perched on the ruffles of raddiatore or nestled in the hollows of little pasta shells. Its colors are as bright as those of an Italian flag, its flavors as fresh as spring.

1 pound shaped pasta, such as shells, wagon wheels, or raddiatore

1 tablespoon olive oil

1 tablespoon unsalted butter

$1/2$ medium onion, chopped

4 plum tomatoes, stemmed and diced

1 clove garlic, minced

One 10-ounce package frozen baby peas or $1 1/4$ pounds fresh baby peas, shelled

$1/2$ cup light cream

2 tablespoons chopped fresh basil

Salt and freshly ground black pepper to taste

Bring a large pot of lightly salted water to a boil. Add the pasta and stir a few times to ensure that the pasta does not stick to itself. Boil vigorously for the time recommended on the pasta package or until the pasta is tender.

While the pasta cooks, heat the olive oil and butter in a large skillet over medium-high heat, add the onion, and cook until softened, about 2 minutes. Add the tomatoes and garlic, cook for 2 minutes, then add the peas and cook for 2 more minutes. Stir in the cream and cook for another 2 minutes. Add the basil, salt, and pepper, and stir to combine the ingredients.

Drain the pasta and toss with the sauce in a serving bowl.

Pecorino Spinach Sauce

**Makes
4 servings**

Romano cheese is made from sheep's milk, and the name Pecorino refers to that heritage. Romano cheese labeled Pecorino is usually imported and is less acrid than domestic Romanos. It is more assertive than Parmesan and not as sweet. Here it gilds a simple plate of pasta and barely blanched spinach. To save on cleanup, the spinach cooks for a few seconds right in the pasta pot.

1 pound pasta, any type
1/4 cup extra-virgin olive oil
2 cloves garlic, minced
Finely grated zest of 1 lemon
Salt to taste

Pinch of cayenne pepper
Two 10-ounce bags fresh spinach, stemmed and washed
1/4 cup finely grated Pecorino Romano cheese

Bring a large pot of lightly salted water to a boil. Add the pasta and stir a few times to ensure that the pasta does not stick to itself. Boil vigorously for the time recommended on the pasta package or until the pasta is tender.

While the pasta cooks, heat the oil in a small skillet over medium heat until hot. Remove from the heat and stir in the garlic, lemon zest, salt, and cayenne. Set aside.

When the pasta is a minute from being finished, add the spinach leaves to the pasta pot and stir just enough to submerge all the spinach. Cook for a minute and drain.

Toss the spinach and pasta with the garlic-oil mixture and the cheese in a serving bowl.

Three-Pepper Sauce

**Makes
4 servings**

This sauce highlights the diverse characteristics of peppers—sweet, pungent, and fiery—by using fresh bell peppers, roasted peppers, and bits of hot jalapeño peppers. After chopping the jalapeños, wash your hands thoroughly with plenty of hot soapy water to rid your fingers of any hot pepper oil that may irritate your skin. The roasted pepper can come from a jar or be homemade. Directions for roasting peppers are on page xix.

1 pound pasta, any shape

$\frac{1}{4}$ cup extra-virgin olive oil

1 large onion, chopped

2 red or yellow bell peppers, stemmed, seeded, and cut in medium dice

1 or 2 jalapeño peppers, stemmed, seeded, and finely diced

5 ounces jarred roasted red peppers, cut into medium dice, or 2 roasted red peppers (see page xix), seeded and cut into medium dice

$\frac{1}{4}$ teaspoon dried oregano

2 cloves garlic, minced

3 tablespoons chopped fresh basil

Salt and freshly ground black pepper to taste

Freshly grated Parmesan cheese (optional)

Bring a large pot of lightly salted water to a boil. Add the pasta and stir a few times to ensure that the pasta does not stick to itself. Boil vigorously for the time recommended on the pasta package or until the pasta is tender.

While the pasta cooks, heat the olive oil in a large skillet over medium-high heat, add the onion, and cook for 1 minute. Add the bell peppers and the jalapeños and cook for 4 minutes, stirring frequently. Add the roasted peppers, oregano, and garlic and cook for 1 minute. Stir in the basil and $\frac{1}{2}$ cup of the pasta water, bring to a boil, and season with salt and pepper.

Drain the pasta and toss with the sauce in a serving bowl. Pass the grated cheese, if desired, at the table.

Summer Squash and Pepper Cheese Sauce

Makes 4 servings

This lemony sauce of shredded zucchini and yellow summer squash practically prepares itself. All you have to do is rid the squash of some of its water before you start cooking. It's easy enough. Since most of the liquid in a squash surrounds its seeds, shred the squash lengthwise, stopping before you hit the center core of seeds.

---

1 pound fettuccine or linguine

2 medium yellow summer squash, ends removed

2 medium zucchini, ends removed

¼ cup extra-virgin olive oil

1 large onion, chopped

2 cloves garlic, minced

1 tablespoon fresh rosemary leaves

Salt and freshly ground black pepper to taste

8 ounces pepper-flavored cheese (feta, chèvre, or brie), crumbled

---

Bring a large pot of lightly salted water to a boil. Add the pasta and stir a few times to ensure that the pasta does not stick to itself. Boil vigorously for the time recommended on the pasta package or until the pasta is tender.

While the pasta cooks, shred the squash and zucchini on the large teeth of a grater. Grate both ends, stopping before you see seeds, then hold the vegetable lengthwise and shred until you get to the center core of seeds; turn the vegetable and continue shredding lengthwise, again stopping before you hit the seeds.

Heat the olive oil in a large skillet over high heat, add the onion, and cook for 1 minute. Add the shredded squash and zucchini, garlic, and rosemary and cook just until the squash softens, 1 to 2 minutes, stirring constantly. Season liberally with salt and pepper.

Drain the pasta and toss it with the sauce and crumbled cheese in a serving bowl.

Chapter 7

Cheese Sauces

Ricotta and Roasted Red Pepper Sauce

Romano, Anchovy, and Garlic Sauce

Carbonara Sauce

Chèvre and Greens Sauce

Cheddar, Ham, and Broccoli Sauce

Gorgonzola and Onion Sauce

Feta, Eggplant, and Olive Sauce

Parmesan, Mushroom, and Tomato Sauce

Four-Cheese Sauce Stunned with Garlic

Fontina Sauce

Cheese is about all that plain pasta needs. Cheeses are naturally pungent and quietly creamy, so their magic can flow into a myriad of sauces with only a little warmth. *And I do mean a little*. Nothing is more destructive to cheese than unbridled fire.

Each cheese family behaves differently, as I explain in more detail on pages xvi–xvii. But for the recipes in this chapter, dry grating cheeses—Parmesan, Romano, and Asiago being the most popular and familiar—are the kind that melt best on pasta. The melting is almost always the last step and is usually done off the heat.

Parmesan, Romano, and Asiago cheeses don't contain enough water to cause the cheese to separate, are high enough in fat to melt on contact with hot noodles, and have sufficiently concentrated flavor to maintain their intensity even when spread over a pile of pasta. All they need is a little oil, a counterpoint of garlic, and a bit of chopped herb.

Dry cheeses also store exceptionally well. Their low moisture content does not readily support the growth of mold and bacteria. Long shelf life has helped make the marketing of grated cheese, especially Parmesan, very profitable, but that has come at the expense of quality.

What most Americans call Parmesan is a far cry from the real thing in Italian cooking. Parmigiano Reggiano, the silken sweet, pungent powder of Emilia-Romano, has little in common with the sharp, acrid, shredded talc that passes for Parmesan cheese in this country. If you've tasted only Parmesan sprinkled from that green shaker, you are in for a real surprise.

Real Parmesan has a natural nutty sweetness and only the faintest hint of salt. Unlike domestic Parmesan, it melts into a buttery glaze, and although it is best when freshly grated, pregrated imported Parmesan will retain its quality in the refrigerator for several months.

Romano, which is made from sheep's milk, has similar textural qualities to Parmesan, although it is more assertive, a bit more acidic, and much more pungent. Many people blend the two, believing that the Parmesan will smooth out the rough edges of the Romano, and that the Romano will give the Parmesan more punch.

Asiago is a cow's-milk cheese with a flavor that falls somewhere between that of Parmesan and Romano.

Ricotta and Roasted Red Pepper Sauce

**Makes
4 servings**

Ricotta cheese is a miraculous substance. Creamy, dairy-rich, and naturally low in fat, it is an instant pasta sauce all by itself. In this recipe, there isn't even any cooking of the sauce. The ricotta is mixed with grated cheese, garlic, roasted peppers, and basil and is set in a bowl of hot water to remove its chill. The hot pasta does the rest.

1 pound pasta, any shape

1 cup part-skim ricotta cheese

3 tablespoons olive oil

7 tablespoons freshly grated Parmesan
  and/or Romano cheese

2 cloves garlic, minced

3 roasted red peppers, jarred or homemade
  (page xix), stemmed, seeded, and diced

1/3 cup chopped fresh basil

Salt and freshly ground black pepper to taste

Bring a large pot of lightly salted water to a boil. Add the pasta and stir a few times to ensure that the pasta does not stick to itself. Boil vigorously for the time recommended on the pasta package or until the pasta is tender.

While the pasta cooks, combine the ricotta, oil, grated cheese, garlic, roasted red peppers, basil, salt, and pepper in a serving bowl. Set the bowl in a larger pan or bowl of boiling water.

Drain the pasta and toss it with the sauce, adding more salt and pepper if needed. Remove the serving bowl from the pan of water, dry its outside, and serve.

Romano, Anchovy, and Garlic Sauce

Makes 4 servings

This perfectly simple sauce is derived from the ancient Roman dip called bagna cauda. Made from anchovies, garlic, and oil, it relies on the pungency of its ingredients and very gentle heating. The anchovy oil is tossed with hot pasta and a generous portion of Romano cheese. Romano is a hard-grating sheep's-milk cheese that, unlike Parmesan, is sharp enough to stand up to the intensity of the anchovies.

1 pound pasta, any shape

6 tablespoons extra-virgin olive oil

4 cloves garlic, minced

One 2-ounce tin flat anchovy fillets packed in olive oil, drained and finely chopped

Pinch of crushed red pepper flakes

2 tablespoons chopped fresh Italian (flat-leaf) parsley

6 tablespoons freshly grated Romano cheese

Salt and freshly ground black pepper to taste (optional)

Bring a large pot of lightly salted water to a boil. Add the pasta and stir a few times to ensure that the pasta does not stick to itself. Boil vigorously for the time recommended on the pasta package or until the pasta is tender.

While the pasta cooks, combine the oil and garlic in a small skillet. Cook over medium heat until you can smell the garlic strongly, about 1 to 2 minutes. Add the anchovies and stir until they soften, about 30 seconds. Remove from the heat and mix in the red pepper flakes and the parsley.

Drain the pasta and toss it in a serving bowl with the sauce and cheese, seasoning with salt and pepper if needed.

Carbonara Sauce

**Makes
4 servings**

Carbonara, one of the simplest and most elegant pasta sauces, is a sophisticated combination of cured meat, egg, and cheese that's traditionally made with pancetta, a rolled unsmoked bacon. Because pancetta is so perishable, it is not sold in most areas of the country, so I've substituted the more commonly available smoked bacon. But if you have a source for real pancetta, use 3 ounces of it and a little olive oil instead of the bacon. Also, you won't need to cook the pancetta quite as long. (This recipe's method of heating cannot guarantee that all bacteria in the egg yolk will be killed. If you are unsure of the safety of your eggs, you might want to skip this recipe.)

---

1 pound pasta, any shape

4 slices bacon, finely chopped

2 egg yolks

1 tablespoon extra-virgin olive oil

2 cloves garlic, minced

Pinch of crushed red pepper flakes

$1/2$ cup freshly grated Parmesan cheese

Salt and freshly ground black pepper to taste

Bring a large pot of lightly salted water to a boil. Add the pasta and stir a few times to ensure that the pasta does not stick to itself. Boil vigorously for the time recommended on the pasta package or until the pasta is tender.

While the pasta cooks, cook the bacon in a skillet over medium heat, stirring often, until it crisps, about 5 minutes. Meanwhile, mix the egg yolks in a serving bowl. Remove the bacon from the heat and stir in the oil, garlic, and red pepper flakes. Slowly pour the contents of the pan into the egg yolks, stirring constantly until the yolks are thick and creamy.

Drain the pasta and toss it in the serving bowl with the sauce and the cheese and season with salt and pepper.

Chèvre and Greens Sauce

**Makes
4 servings**

The appeal of chèvre (goat cheese) and greens is an attraction of opposites: soft and crisp, mild and sharp, plump and lean. This recipe is a play on the country French pairing of fresh goat cheese and endive lettuce. Cooking the endive emphasizes its fresh flavor and provocative bitter overtones.

---

1 pound pasta, any shape

¼ cup extra-virgin olive oil

2 cloves garlic, minced

¾ pound endive or escarole, stemmed, cored, and washed

Salt and freshly ground black pepper to taste

1 small package (about 5 ounces) fresh chèvre, crumbled

Bring a large pot of lightly salted water to a boil. Add the pasta and stir a few times to ensure that the pasta does not stick to itself. Boil vigorously for the time recommended on the pasta package or until the pasta is tender.

While the pasta cooks, heat the oil in a large, deep, nonstick skillet over medium-high heat. Add the garlic and greens, stirring until the greens wilt, about 3 minutes. Season liberally with salt and pepper.

Drain the pasta and toss it in a serving bowl with the sautéed greens and chèvre, adding more salt and pepper if needed.

Cheddar, Ham, and Broccoli Sauce

**Makes
4 servings**

This classic trio makes a delicious pasta sauce. The broccoli is cooked right along with the pasta, and the ham is heated just enough to bring out its familiar combination of sweet, salt, and smoke. The cheese is added at the end, melted only by the heat of the pasta.

1 pound pasta, any shape

1 bunch broccoli florets, cut in bite-size pieces

2 tablespoons olive oil

1 medium onion, chopped

6 ounces smoked ham, cut in small dice

2 cloves garlic, minced

Salt and freshly ground black pepper
  to taste

2 cups shredded sharp Cheddar cheese
  (about 8 ounces)

Bring a large pot of lightly salted water to a boil. Add the pasta and stir a few times to ensure that the pasta does not stick to itself. Boil vigorously for the time recommended on the pasta package or until the pasta is tender. Two minutes before the pasta will finish cooking, add the broccoli florets and stir.

While the pasta cooks, heat the oil in a large, deep, nonstick skillet over medium-high heat. Add the onion and ham and cook, stirring, until the onion has softened, about 2 minutes. Add the garlic and season liberally with salt and pepper.

Drain the pasta and broccoli and toss them in a serving bowl with the sautéed ingredients and the cheese, adding more salt and pepper if needed.

Gorgonzola and Onion Sauce

**Makes
4 servings**

Of all the noble blue cheeses, Gorgonzola is the sweetest, mildest, creamiest, and easiest to love. Here its gentleness is underscored by teaming it with the sweetest of sweet onions. The Vidalias melt into tender threads, which carry the melted cheese over the noodles. The whole is sparked by a hit of sweet balsamic vinegar.

1 pound pasta, any shape

¼ cup olive oil

2 large Vidalia (or other sweet) onions, peeled, quartered, and thinly sliced

2 cloves garlic, minced

2 tablespoons balsamic vinegar

Salt and freshly ground black pepper to taste

4 ounces Gorgonzola cheese, crumbled

Bring a large pot of lightly salted water to a boil. Add the pasta and stir a few times to ensure that the pasta does not stick to itself. Boil vigorously for the time recommended on the pasta package or until the pasta is tender.

While the pasta cooks, heat the oil in a large, deep, nonstick skillet over medium-high heat. Add the onions and cook, stirring often, until they have become very soft and golden brown, about 5 minutes. Add the garlic and cook 1 more minute. Remove from the heat and stir in the balsamic vinegar, salt, and pepper.

Drain the pasta and toss it in a serving bowl with the sautéed onions and the Gorgonzola, adding more salt and pepper if needed.

Feta, Eggplant, and Olive Sauce

**Makes
4 servings**

This sauce incorporates the flavors of Greece in a simple sautéed sauce. The only unusual preparation involves precooking the eggplant. Eggplants contain a lot of water, which can overtake the sauce. To rid the vegetable of some of its moisture, it is tossed with a little kosher salt (salt draws moisture from food fibers) and microwaved. Once it has softened, the eggplant is squeezed in a towel to draw out much of its fluid and most of the added salt.

---

1 pound pasta, any shape

1 1/2 pounds small firm eggplant, stemmed, peeled, and cut into thin 2-inch-long strips

1 teaspoon kosher salt

3 tablespoons olive oil

1/2 medium onion, chopped

Pinch of crushed red pepper flakes

1/2 teaspoon dried oregano

3 cloves garlic, minced

1/4 cup chopped fresh basil

12 imported black olives (Mislinis, Kalamata, or Niçoise), pitted and coarsely chopped

4 ounces feta cheese, crumbled

Bring a large pot of lightly salted water to a boil. Add the pasta and stir a few times to ensure that the pasta does not stick to itself. Boil vigorously for the time recommended on the pasta package or until the pasta is tender.

While the pasta cooks, toss the eggplant with the kosher salt in a microwave-safe dish. Cover and microwave at full power for 2 minutes. Transfer to a clean kitchen towel and squeeze out the excess water.

Heat the oil in a medium nonstick skillet over medium-high heat. Add the onion and red pepper flakes and cook until the onion has softened, about 2 minutes. Add the oregano and eggplant and cook until the eggplant has lightly browned, about 3 minutes. Stir in the garlic, basil, and olives.

Drain the pasta and toss it in a serving bowl with the sauce and cheese.

Parmesan, Mushroom, and Tomato Sauce

Makes 4 servings

Pasta sauces don't come any more straightforward than this—sautéed mushrooms, garlic, tomatoes, and a pile of Parmesan.

1 pound pasta, any shape

1/4 cup olive oil

1 medium onion, chopped

3/4 pound medium mushrooms, cleaned, stemmed, and sliced

2 teaspoons fresh thyme

2 cloves garlic, minced

4 plum tomatoes, stemmed and chopped

Salt and freshly ground black pepper to taste

2 tablespoons chopped fresh Italian (flat-leaf) parsley

6 tablespoons freshly grated Parmesan cheese

Bring a large pot of lightly salted water to a boil. Add the pasta and stir a few times to ensure that the pasta does not stick to itself. Boil vigorously for the time recommended on the pasta package or until the pasta is tender.

While the pasta cooks, heat the oil in a large heavy skillet over medium-high heat, add the onion, and cook for 1 minute. Add the mushrooms and cook until they lose their raw look, about 2 minutes. Add the thyme, garlic, tomatoes, salt, and pepper and cook until the tomatoes soften, about 3 minutes. If the mixture becomes too dry, add up to 1/2 cup of the pasta cooking water. Stir in the parsley.

Drain the pasta and toss it in a serving bowl with the sauce and the cheese, adding more salt and pepper if needed.

Four-Cheese Sauce Stunned with Garlic

**Makes
4 servings**

The trick to this sauce is to have all the cheeses in the smallest pieces possible, because the only heat that will melt them comes from the pasta. Of the four cheeses, the one that might be unfamiliar to you is ricotta salata. *This very plain, dry, white cheese is a slightly aged ricotta. If you can't find it, substitute feta or farmer cheese.*

---

1 pound pasta, any shape

1/4 cup olive oil

4 cloves garlic, minced

2 tablespoons chopped fresh Italian (flat-leaf) parsley

Salt and freshly ground black pepper to taste

2 ounces provolone cheese, shredded

2 ounces *ricotta salata*, crumbled

3 tablespoons freshly grated Parmesan cheese

3 tablespoons freshly grated Romano cheese

Bring a large pot of lightly salted water to a boil. Add the pasta and stir a few times to ensure that the pasta does not stick to itself. Boil vigorously for the time recommended on the pasta package or until the pasta is tender.

While the pasta cooks, heat the oil in a medium skillet over medium-high heat. Remove from the heat and stir in the garlic, parsley, salt, and pepper. Add 1/2 cup of the pasta cooking water.

Drain the pasta and toss it in a serving bowl with the garlic mixture and the cheeses, adding more salt and pepper if needed.

Fontina Sauce

**Makes
4 servings**

This sauce is made similarly to fondue. Italian fontina, a wonderful creamy, nutty, smoky melting cheese, is tossed with a little cornstarch. An unthickened wine sauce is prepared and the cheese is whisked into the sauce, off the heat. The cornstarch helps thicken the sauce, and the lack of direct flame keeps the cheese from curdling.

---

1 pound fettuccine

6 ounces Italian fontina cheese, rind removed and finely chopped or shredded

1 tablespoon cornstarch

2 tablespoons olive oil

1/2 medium onion, finely chopped

2 cloves garlic, minced

Pinch of cayenne pepper

1 1/2 cups dry white wine

Salt and freshly ground black pepper to taste

2 tablespoons finely chopped fresh Italian (flat-leaf) parsley

---

Bring a large pot of lightly salted water to a boil. Add the pasta and stir a few times to ensure that the pasta does not stick to itself. Boil vigorously for the time recommended on the pasta package or until the pasta is tender.

While the pasta cooks, toss the fontina with the cornstarch and set aside. Heat the oil in a medium skillet over medium-high heat, add the onion, and cook until softened, about 2 minutes. Add the garlic and cayenne and stir. Add the wine and boil vigorously for 1 minute. Season with salt and pepper.

Just before the pasta is ready, bring the sauce back to a boil. Remove from the heat and whisk in the fontina until the sauce is smooth.

Drain the pasta and toss it in a serving bowl with the sauce and parsley, adding more salt and pepper if needed.

Chapter 8

Stir-Fried Sauces

Stir-Fried Primavera Sauce

Stir-Fried Mushroom Beef Sauce

Stir-Fried Broccoli and Walnut Sauce

Stir-Fried Herbed Mushroom Sauce

Stir-Fried Classic Meat Sauce

Stir-Fried Savory Turkey Sauce

Stir-Fried Kraut and Chicken Liver Sauce

Stir-Fried Pork and Shrimp Sauce

Stir-Fried Herb Chicken Sauce

Stir-Fried Bouillabaisse Sauce

tir-fry refers to a cooking method, not a flavor. But by imprisoning it next to ginger, hoisin, and soy sauce, we have taken a versatile technique and sentenced it to a one-track future.

Think about it. Stir-frying is nothing more than braising in a wok, and it can be a blessing for any dish that starts with a sauté and finishes with a simmer—in other words, pasta sauces. The biggest difference in stir-frying is the intensity of the heat and the speed with which that intense heat cooks food. It's a difference that can give you a great advantage when time is of the essence.

If you don't have a wok and don't want to buy one, you can use a large, deep, heavy-gauged skillet instead, but it will not cook food as quickly or as evenly. Any stir-fry can be made in a skillet. But just as surely, any sauce traditionally made in a sauté pan or a saucepan can be made more easily and more quickly in a wok.

A wok is a wide metal pan with deep sloping sides and a rounded bottom. This design concentrates heat down in the swollen belly of the pan where meat or vegetables can be quickly browned. After browning, liquid can be added. The concentration of heat will bring that liquid to a boil in seconds, and the depth of the wok will ensure that the sauce will not boil over.

Because stir-frying is such a quick method of cooking, all ingredients must be prepared and ready to go before the wok is ever heated. Vegetables should be chopped, meat must be trimmed and sliced, liquids should be measured and mixed, and spices should be laid out on a plate.

Tender vegetables, such as onion, spinach, or cabbage, need only be wilted in hot oil. Stir them as soon as they hit the heat and they will cook through in seconds. On the other hand, meat should sit undisturbed in the bottom of the wok for a minute in order to brown properly. When meat and vegetables are cooked together, one gets added first, is removed, and then is returned when the rest of the ingredients are ready.

At first, Stir-Fried Primavera Sauce or Stir-Fried Meat Sauce may seem a tad eccentric, but once you've stir-fried a sauce or two, you'll come to depend on this commonsense approach for quick, everyday meals.

Stir-Fried Primavera Sauce

**Makes
4 servings**

What could be more mundane than a stir-fry of vegetables? But toss them with olive oil, basil, and Parmesan and this stir-fry turns into an Italian novelty. Novel or not, the speed of the cooking and the wonderful vegetable textures it achieves make it make perfect sense.

1 pound shaped pasta, such as penne
  or bowties

2 tablespoons extra-virgin olive oil

1 medium onion, chopped

4 ounces baby carrots, trimmed and peeled

1/2 yellow bell pepper, cut in strips

1/2 pound thin asparagus, trimmed and
  cut in 1-inch lengths

1 clove garlic, minced

1 cup frozen baby peas (about 5 ounces)

12 cherry tomatoes, halved

1/4 cup chopped fresh basil

Salt and freshly ground black pepper to taste

1/4 cup freshly grated Parmesan or Romano
  cheese

Bring a large pot of lightly salted water to a boil. Add the pasta and stir a few times to ensure that the pasta does not stick to itself. Boil vigorously for the time recommended on the pasta package or until the pasta is tender.

While the pasta cooks, heat the oil in a wok over high heat, add the onion, and cook until softened, about 30 to 60 seconds. Add the carrots and stir to coat with oil. Add 2 tablespoons of the pasta cooking water, cover, and steam for 1 minute. Add the bell pepper and stir-fry for 1 more minute. Add the asparagus and toss. Add 2 more tablespoons of the pasta cooking water, cover, and steam for 1 minute. Add the garlic, peas, tomatoes, basil, salt, and pepper and stir-fry until the peas are warmed through and the tomatoes soften, about 2 minutes.

Drain the pasta and toss it with the sauce and the cheese in a serving bowl. Add more salt and pepper if needed.

Stir-Fried Mushroom Beef Sauce

Although it has two forms of tomatoes in it, this sauce is not a tomato sauce. It is dominated by strips of flank steak and slices of mushroom, and it's glazed with olive oil, herbs, and bits of tomato and onion.

---

1 pound tube-shaped pasta, such as
    penne or ziti

1 pound flank steak, cut in thin strips

Salt and freshly ground black pepper to taste

1/4 cup olive oil

1 medium onion, chopped

3/4 pound mushrooms, cleaned, stemmed,
    and sliced

2 teaspoons fresh thyme leaves

1 clove garlic, minced

2 cups diced tomatoes

1 tablespoon tomato paste

Salt and freshly ground black pepper to taste

1 teaspoon balsamic vinegar

Bring a large pot of lightly salted water to a boil. Add the pasta and stir a few times to ensure that the pasta does not stick to itself. Boil vigorously for the time recommended on the pasta package or until the pasta is tender.

While the pasta cooks, season the flank steak with salt and pepper. Heat half of the oil in a wok over high heat, add the flank steak, and stir-fry until meat is uniformly brown, about 2 minutes. Remove to a plate.

Heat the remaining oil in the wok, add the onion, and cook until softened, about 30 to 60 seconds. Add the mushrooms, toss to coat with oil, add 1 tablespoon water, and continue stir-frying until the mushrooms lose their raw look.

Return the beef to the wok, add the thyme and garlic, and stir-fry 1 minute. Add the tomatoes and tomato paste and stir-fry 1 minute more. Season with salt and pepper and stir in the vinegar.

Drain the pasta and toss it in a serving bowl with the sauce. Add more salt and pepper if needed.

Stir-Fried Broccoli and Walnut Sauce

Makes 4 servings

The attraction between green vegetables and toasted nuts makes perfect sense. One is lean and full of garden freshness. The other is rich with sweet, aromatic oils and a roasted caramelized flavor.

---

1 pound pasta, any shape

2 tablespoons olive oil

3/4 cup chopped walnuts

2 cloves garlic, minced

Salt and freshly ground black pepper to taste

1 bunch broccoli florets, cut in bite-size pieces

Pinch of crushed red pepper flakes

2 tablespoons walnut oil

2 tablespoons freshly grated Romano cheese

Bring a large pot of lightly salted water to a boil. Add the pasta and stir a few times to ensure that the pasta does not stick to itself. Boil vigorously for the time recommended on the pasta package or until the pasta is tender.

While the pasta cooks, heat half the olive oil in a wok over high heat. Add the walnuts and stir-fry until lightly toasted, about 45 seconds. Remove with a slotted spoon to a serving bowl and toss with half the garlic, the salt, and the pepper.

Heat the remaining olive oil in the wok, add the broccoli and the red pepper flakes, and stir-fry until the broccoli turns bright green. Add the remaining garlic, more salt and pepper, and 1/3 cup of water. Cover and steam until the broccoli is tender, about 3 minutes, uncover, and continue cooking until the remaining water has evaporated.

Drain the pasta, toss it in the bowl with the walnuts, and add the broccoli mixture, walnut oil, and cheese. Add more salt and pepper if needed.

Stir-Fried Herbed Mushroom Sauce

**Makes
4 servings**

This sauce is all mushroom. No tomato or cream to cloud the issue, just mushroom slices, herbs, and a clean squeeze of lemon juice to brighten the finish. Don't worry about the lack of liquid. Mushrooms are loaded with flavorful juices that will build as the sauce cooks.

---

1 pound pasta, any shape

2 tablespoons extra-virgin olive oil

1/2 medium onion, chopped

1 1/2 pounds medium mushrooms, cleaned, stemmed, and sliced

Salt and freshly ground black pepper to taste

1 tablespoon chopped fresh herbs (rosemary, chive, thyme, dill, etc.)

2 tablespoons chopped fresh Italian (flat-leaf) parsley

Juice of 1/2 lemon

2 tablespoons freshly grated Parmesan or Romano cheese

Bring a large pot of lightly salted water to a boil. Add the pasta and stir a few times to ensure that the pasta does not stick to itself. Boil vigorously for the time recommended on the pasta package or until the pasta is tender.

While the pasta cooks, heat the olive oil in a wok over high heat, add the onion, and stir-fry until softened, about 30 to 60 seconds. Add the mushrooms, salt, and pepper and continue stir-frying until the edges of some of the mushrooms begin to brown slightly. Add the herbs, parsley, and 1/2 cup of the pasta cooking water and boil for 1 minute. Remove from the heat and stir in the lemon juice.

Drain the pasta and toss it with the sauce and cheese in a serving bowl. Add more salt and pepper if needed.

Stir-Fried Classic Meat Sauce

**Makes
4 servings**

This is as straightforward as a pasta sauce can get. It is an everyday basic meat sauce, but its one distinction is that it's made in a wok, which means it comes together almost as fast as you can open a jar.

1 pound pasta, any shape
2 tablespoons olive oil
1 medium onion, chopped
1 pound ground beef
2 cloves garlic, minced

Pinch of crushed red pepper flakes
One 28-ounce can crushed tomatoes
$1/4$ cup chopped fresh basil
Salt and freshly ground black pepper to taste

Bring a large pot of lightly salted water to a boil. Add the pasta and stir a few times to ensure that the pasta does not stick to itself. Boil vigorously for the time recommended on the pasta package or until the pasta is tender.

While the pasta cooks, heat the oil in a wok over high heat, add the onion, and cook until softened, about 30 to 60 seconds. Add the ground beef, stirring and breaking up the meat until it loses its raw look, about 1 minute. Add the garlic and the red pepper flakes and stir-fry for 30 seconds more. Stir in the tomatoes and simmer for 3 minutes. Add the basil, salt, and pepper and simmer another minute.

Drain the pasta and toss with the sauce in a serving bowl. Add more salt and pepper if needed.

Stir-Fried Savory Turkey Sauce

**Makes
4 servings**

*Turkey breast, simmered into a savory stew, is tossed with potatoes and pasta,
creating a dish that's as close to Thanksgiving dinner as pasta is likely to get.
The potatoes are cooked with the pasta to save time, and their starch coats the
noodles while it lightly thickens the sauce.*

---

1 pound pasta, any shape

³/₄ pound red-skin potatoes, peeled and
   cut in medium dice

2 tablespoons olive oil

1 medium onion, chopped

1 pound boneless, skinless turkey
   breast, cubed

2 cloves garlic, minced

¹/₂ cup dry white wine

1 cup chicken broth

15 chives, sliced

2 tablespoons chopped fresh Italian
   (flat-leaf) parsley

2 tablespoons butter

Salt and freshly ground black pepper
   to taste

Bring a large pot of lightly salted water to a boil. Add the pasta and the potatoes and stir a few times to ensure that the pasta does not stick to itself. Boil
vigorously for the time recommended on the pasta package or until the pasta
is tender.

While the pasta cooks, heat the oil in a wok over high heat, add the onion,
and cook until softened, about 30 to 60 seconds. Add the turkey and stir-fry
until it loses its raw look. Add the garlic and wine and boil for 1 minute. Add
the chicken broth and cook until the liquid reduces by half.

A minute before the pasta finishes cooking, add the chives and parsley to
the wok, along with about 8 pieces of cooked potato from the pasta pot. Mash
the potato with the back of your stir-frying tool, remove from the heat, and mix
in the butter.

Drain the pasta and potatoes and toss them with the sauce in a serving
bowl. Season with salt and pepper.

Stir-Fried Kraut and Chicken Liver Sauce

**Makes
4 servings**

Cabbage, often seen as the blandest of vegetables, takes on a rich toasted patina in the heat of a wok. This recipe underscores those flavors with sautéed chicken livers. I know that liver is hardly anyone's favorite food, but I insist that's because most people cook it so poorly. Don't overcook the chicken livers. Too much heat makes them grainy, bitter, and (for lack of a better word) livery. As soon as they are firm, they are done.

1 pound shaped pasta, such as elbows
or wagon wheels

2 tablespoons olive or vegetable oil

3/4 pound chicken livers, trimmed and
cut in large chunks

1 large onion, chopped

2 cloves garlic, minced

1/2 head white cabbage, quartered
and thinly sliced

1 teaspoon ground ginger

Salt and freshly ground black
pepper to taste

Bring a large pot of lightly salted water to a boil. Add the pasta and stir a few times to ensure that the pasta does not stick to itself. Boil vigorously for the time recommended on the pasta package or until the pasta is tender.

While the pasta cooks, heat the oil in a wok over high heat. Add the livers, cook until they lose their raw look, and transfer them to a bowl using a slotted spoon.

Add the onion to the oil remaining in the pan and stir-fry until softened, about 30 to 60 seconds. Add the garlic, cabbage, ginger, salt, and pepper and stir-fry for 3 to 4 minutes, until the cabbage is soft and lightly browned. Return the livers to the pan and continue cooking until they are firm, about 2 more minutes.

Drain the pasta and toss it with the sauce in a serving bowl. Add more salt and pepper if needed.

Stir-Fried Pork and Shrimp Sauce

**Makes
4 servings**

I couldn't do a stir-fry chapter without succumbing to the Asian connection. Shrimp and pork are traditional mates in Chinese cooking. In this recipe, they are glazed with the four standard-bearers of Chinese cooking—soy sauce, ginger, garlic, and sesame oil. It's a great combination. So who am I to buck tradition?

1 pound shaped pasta, such as raddiatore or bowties

2 tablespoons vegetable oil

1 medium onion, chopped

One 1-inch piece fresh ginger, peeled and cut in thin strips

8 ounces boneless pork chop, cut in 1-inch cubes

Pinch of crushed red pepper flakes

2 cloves garlic, minced

$3/4$ cup chicken broth

$1/2$ pound medium shrimp (31–35 count), peeled and deveined

1 cup mung bean sprouts

1 tablespoon soy sauce

2 tablespoons dry sherry

1 teaspoon dark sesame oil

Salt and freshly ground black pepper to taste

Bring a large pot of lightly salted water to a boil. Add the pasta and stir a few times to ensure that the pasta does not stick to itself. Boil vigorously for the time recommended on the pasta package or until the pasta is tender.

While the pasta cooks, heat the oil in a wok over high heat, add the onion and ginger, and stir-fry until the onion softens, about 30 to 60 seconds. Add the pork and stir-fry until lightly browned, about 3 minutes. Add the red pepper flakes, garlic, and chicken broth and boil for 1 minute. Add the shrimp, sprouts, soy sauce, and sherry and boil for 45 seconds. Stir in the sesame oil, salt, and pepper.

Drain the pasta and toss it with the sauce in a serving bowl. Add more salt and pepper if needed.

Stir-Fried Herb Chicken Sauce

**Makes
4 servings**

This light tomato sauce has been bulked up with chicken and perfumed with the classic herb combination of rosemary and sage.

---

1 pound pasta, any shape

¼ cup extra-virgin olive oil

1 medium onion, chopped

1 pound boneless, skinless
   chicken breast, cubed

1 sprig fresh rosemary

1 sprig fresh sage

2 cloves garlic, diced

½ cup diced tomato

1 cup dry white wine

½ cup chicken broth

Salt and freshly ground black pepper to taste

Bring a large pot of lightly salted water to a boil. Add the pasta and stir a few times to ensure that the pasta does not stick to itself. Boil vigorously for the time recommended on the pasta package or until the pasta is tender.

While the pasta cooks, heat the oil in a wok over high heat, add the onion, and cook until softened, about 30 to 60 seconds. Add the chicken and stir-fry until it loses its raw look. Add the whole sprigs of rosemary and sage and the garlic, tomato, wine, and chicken broth. Boil for 3 minutes, until the chicken is done and the broth is flavored with the herbs. Remove and discard the herbs.

Drain the pasta and toss it in a serving bowl with the sauce. Add salt and pepper.

Stir-Fried Bouillabaisse Sauce

**Makes
4 servings**

This fish sauce for pasta has all the flavors of coastal Provence—fennel, orange, tomato, basil, garlic, and onion. The intensity of the ingredients helps the broth to form in minutes, and the fish takes just a moment to poach. The results are that odd combination of strong ethnic flavor in a dish that is multidimensional and sophisticated.

1 pound shell-shaped pasta

2 tablespoons extra-virgin olive oil

1 medium onion, chopped

2 teaspoons fennel seed, ground

2 cloves garlic, minced

1 cup dry white wine

Zest and juice of 1 orange, zest chopped
  or cut in thin strips

1 tablespoon chopped fresh basil

$1/2$ cup crushed tomatoes in purée

$1/2$ cup diced tomatoes, fresh or canned

Salt and freshly ground black pepper to taste

1 pound firm-flesh fish, such as swordfish,
  tuna, roughy, or St. Peter's

Bring a large pot of lightly salted water to a boil. Add the pasta and stir a few times to ensure that the pasta does not stick to itself. Boil vigorously for the time recommended on the pasta package or until the pasta is tender.

While the pasta cooks, heat the olive oil in a wok over high heat, add the onion, and stir-fry until softened, about 30 to 60 seconds. Add the fennel seed and garlic and stir-fry another 30 seconds. Stir in the wine and bring to a boil. Add the orange zest, basil, crushed and diced tomatoes, salt, and pepper and boil for 2 minutes. Add the fish and simmer for 2 minutes. Stir in the orange juice.

Drain the pasta and toss it with the sauce in a serving bowl. Add more salt and pepper if needed.

Chapter 9

Uncooked Sauces

Tomato Basil Salsa

Anchovy Aïoli

Roquefort, Spinach, and Garlic Sauce

Niçoise Sauce

Tomato, Artichoke, and Feta Sauce

Olive Pepper Salsa

Arugula, Prosciutto, and Aged Ricotta Sauce

Herbed Alfredo Sauce

Smoked Salmon, Asparagus, and Lemon Ricotta Sauce

Sun-Dried Tomato Paste

Long-simmered pasta sauces are so commonplace that we often forget the flavorful possibilities of fresh vegetables tossed simply with bright green herbs, a little oil, and piping-hot noodles. Especially as temperatures outside start to heat up, the ease, natural flavors, and stove-free preparation of uncooked pasta sauces make them essential for any summer cook who can't stand the heat but is still stuck in the kitchen.

Heat doesn't just cook food, it also brings out its flavor. So when we abandon the stove, we must make up for the potential flavor loss.

Quality ingredients are essential. Less-than-perfect tomatoes in a *cooked* sauce can be overcome with a jolt of tomato paste or a swirl of cream, but in a *raw* sauce, the tomato must stand on its own merits. You can complement it with garlic, hot pepper, or cheese, but if the tomato doesn't have what it takes, your sauce won't either.

Because you can't rely on heat to blend and marry the flavors of an uncooked sauce, take advantage of the large number of high-quality precooked processed products available to you. Combining a jar of marinated artichokes, some smoked salmon, or a tin of anchovies with other fresh ingredients can give you the multidimensional flavor of a cooked sauce without the loss of the vibrant color and texture of fresh herbs and vegetables that excessive heat can cause.

Cooking isn't the only way to enliven flavor. Chopping accomplishes the same thing, and the more finely an ingredient is chopped, the more its flavors emerge. That's why a clove of garlic reveals barely a hint of itself when simmered whole in a stew or broth but becomes quite pungent when minced. The same holds true for herbs, vegetables, and aromatic seasonings like ginger and peppers.

Pay close attention to the texture of your ingredients. Finely chop crunchy ingredients, like cucumber, peppers, fennel, or walnuts, for a subtle textural variation in the sauce. Soft vegetables, such as tomatoes, zucchini, spinach, and herb leaves, can be left in bigger pieces, but at no time should the sauce ingredients be chunkier than bite-size. Softer vegetables can be puréed in a food processor, but be careful about chopping crunchy vegetables too finely. Without the benefit of cooking to soften their tough fibers, minute pieces of raw celery or carrot can give an unpleasant sandy texture to a sauce.

Tomato Basil Salsa

**Makes
4 servings**

Salsa is not just for chips. This one delivers all the flavor of a classic Italian tomato sauce with none of the work. It is best made with very ripe beefsteak tomatoes, which have the depth of flavor and the meaty texture you need. If you need to substitute another type of tomato, go ahead, but make sure it's very ripe. If all you have are pallid winter tomatoes, forget this sauce altogether.

---

1 pound curly or shaped pasta, such as rotelle or shells

1 small onion, quartered

3 large beefsteak tomatoes, stemmed and coarsely chopped

2 cloves garlic

24 fresh basil leaves

1/4 teaspoon crushed red pepper flakes

2 tablespoons olive oil

2 tablespoons chopped fresh Italian (flat-leaf) parsley

Salt and freshly ground black pepper to taste

Freshly grated Parmesan cheese (optional)

Bring a large pot of lightly salted water to a boil. Add the pasta and stir a few times to ensure that the pasta does not stick to itself. Boil vigorously for the time recommended on the pasta package or until the pasta is tender.

While the pasta cooks, finely chop the onion, tomatoes, garlic, and basil leaves in a blender or food processor or with a knife. In a serving bowl large enough to hold the pasta, combine the chopped ingredients, red pepper flakes, olive oil, parsley, salt, and pepper.

Drain the pasta and toss it thoroughly in the bowl with the sauce. Serve with Parmesan cheese if desired.

Anchovy Aïoli

**Makes
4 servings**

Aïoli, the garlic mayonnaise of Provence, is typically served with grilled and poached meats, fish, and poultry. In this recipe, the mayonnaise is infused with anchovies for a deceptively rich and pungent pasta sauce. (And with a little more vinegar, it makes a great dressing for pasta salad.)

---

1 pound pasta, any shape

One 2-ounce tin flat anchovy fillets
packed in olive oil

4 cloves garlic, minced

¼ cup mayonnaise

2 tablespoons extra-virgin olive oil

1 teaspoon balsamic vinegar

2 tablespoons chopped fresh dill or
Italian (flat-leaf) parsley

Freshly ground black pepper to taste

Bring a large pot of lightly salted water to a boil. Add the pasta and stir a few times to ensure that the pasta does not stick to itself. Boil vigorously for the time recommended on the pasta package or until the pasta is tender.

While the pasta cooks, mince the anchovies and reserve the oil in which they are packed. In a serving bowl, mix the anchovies, garlic, and mayonnaise into as smooth a paste as possible. Mix in the olive oil and the oil from the anchovies a little at a time. Mix in the vinegar, dill or parsley, and pepper.

Drain the pasta and toss it in the bowl with the sauce.

Roquefort, Spinach, and Garlic Sauce

**Makes
4 servings**

Ingredients of unbridled flavor are essential for sauces that don't get the benefit of heat, and no one could ask for a better start than Roquefort cheese. The only blue-veined cheese made from sheep's milk, Roquefort is creamy, tangy, and richly aromatic. Little else is needed but some garlic and a bit of oil. The spinach cooks right in with the pasta.

1 pound long pasta, such as fettuccine or
   spaghetti

2 cloves garlic, minced

6 ounces Roquefort cheese, crumbled

1/4 cup olive oil

Salt and freshly ground black pepper to taste

One 10-ounce bag fresh spinach, stemmed
   and washed

Bring a large pot of lightly salted water to a boil. Add the pasta and stir a few times to ensure that the pasta does not stick to itself. Boil vigorously for the time recommended on the pasta package or until the pasta is tender.

While the pasta cooks, mix the garlic, cheese, oil, salt, and pepper in a serving bowl and set aside.

When the pasta is ready, add the spinach leaves to the pasta pot and stir just enough to submerge all the spinach. Cook 10 seconds more and drain the pasta and spinach. Toss the pasta and spinach with the sauce in the bowl.

Niçoise Sauce

**Makes
4 servings**

The cuisine of Nice is dominated by the ingredients of the Riviera—seafood, olives, tomatoes, and garlic. This sauce takes advantage of the entire spectrum, and by using canned tuna, the need for cooking is eliminated. I recommend you use tuna packed in olive oil. It has a much more natural flavor and a moister texture than water-packed tuna, and the packing oil can double as the sauce base.

1 pound curly or shaped pasta, such as rotelle or shells

One 6-ounce can (approximately) tuna packed in oil

12 black olives (preferably oil-cured), pitted and coarsely chopped

4 scallions (white part only), thinly sliced

1 ripe tomato, stemmed and finely chopped

2 cloves garlic, minced

12 fresh basil leaves, chopped

2 tablespoons extra-virgin olive oil

Salt and freshly ground black pepper to taste

3 tablespoons freshly grated Parmesan cheese

Bring a large pot of lightly salted water to a boil. Add the pasta and stir a few times to ensure that the pasta does not stick to itself. Boil vigorously for the time recommended on the pasta package or until the pasta is tender.

While the pasta cooks, place the tuna with its oil in a serving bowl and use a fork to break the tuna into small pieces. Mix the tuna, olives, scallions, tomato, garlic, basil, olive oil, salt, and pepper.

Drain the pasta and toss it in the bowl with the sauce and Parmesan cheese.

Tomato, Artichoke, and Feta Sauce

**Makes
4 servings**

You must have guessed by now that I consider marinated artichoke hearts the greatest convenience ingredient since tomato paste in a tube. Their texture has just the right give, their flavor is subtle, and their marinade is well rounded. Feta cheese is their perfect complement.

1 pound shaped pasta, such as elbows
   or shells

One 6-ounce jar marinated artichoke hearts

1 large tomato, stemmed and finely chopped

2 cloves garlic, minced

Pinch of crushed red pepper flakes

2 tablespoons extra-virgin olive oil

Salt and freshly ground black pepper to taste

7 to 8 ounces feta cheese

3 tablespoons chopped fresh Italian (flat-leaf)
   parsley

Bring a large pot of lightly salted water to a boil. Add the pasta and stir a few times to ensure that the pasta does not stick to itself. Boil vigorously for the time recommended on the pasta package or until the pasta is tender.

While the pasta cooks, chop the artichoke hearts and mix them with the liquid in the jar, the tomato, garlic, red pepper flakes, olive oil, salt, and pepper in a serving bowl.

Drain the pasta and toss it with the mixture in the bowl, along with the feta cheese and the parsley.

Olive Pepper Salsa

**Makes
4 servings**

This very pungent salsa is enriched by meaty, oily olives and extra-virgin olive oil. It uses both black and green olives. Make sure your black olives are imported varieties, such as Kalamata, Mislinis, or Niçoise. Canned California olives are far too bland to give the sauce its due.

---

1 pound curly or shaped pasta, such as raddiatore or rotelle

1/3 cup imported black olives, pitted and chopped

1/3 cup pimiento-stuffed Spanish olives, chopped

1 roasted red bell pepper, jarred or homemade (page xix), diced

4 scallions (white part only), thinly sliced

1 tomato, stemmed and finely chopped

Pinch of dried oregano

6 fresh basil leaves, finely chopped

2 cloves garlic, minced

2 tablespoons extra-virgin olive oil

Salt and freshly ground black pepper to taste

Bring a large pot of lightly salted water to a boil. Add the pasta and stir a few times to ensure that the pasta does not stick to itself. Boil vigorously for the time recommended on the pasta package or until the pasta is tender.

While the pasta cooks, combine the olives, roasted pepper, scallions, tomato, oregano, basil, garlic, oil, salt, and pepper in a pasta serving bowl.

Drain the pasta and toss it in the bowl with the olive sauce.

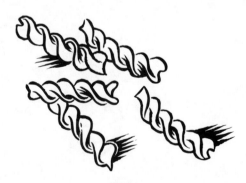

Arugula, Prosciutto, and Aged Ricotta Sauce

**Makes
4 servings**

Arugula is a loose-leafed bitter lettuce. It is excellent with cheese, and it's a highlight in a simple salad of tossed greens. In this recipe, its tangy, slightly peppery punch is balanced by sweet and salty prosciutto and a very low-fat fresh dairy cheese. Aged ricotta, called ricotta salata, *is a firm cheese, much like feta. In fact, if you can't find the aged ricotta, feta makes a fine substitute.*

1 pound pasta, any shape
1 bunch arugula, finely chopped
2 ounces prosciutto, finely chopped
1 clove garlic, finely chopped

5 ounces aged ricotta (*ricotta salata*) or feta cheese, crumbled
Salt and freshly ground black pepper to taste

Bring a large pot of lightly salted water to a boil. Add the pasta and stir a few times to ensure that the pasta does not stick to itself. Boil vigorously for the time recommended on the pasta package or until the pasta is tender.

While the pasta cooks, combine the arugula, prosciutto, garlic, cheese, salt, and pepper in a serving bowl. Stir in ½ cup of the pasta water.

Drain the pasta and toss it in the serving bowl with the arugula mixture.

Herbed Alfredo Sauce

Makes
4 servings

Alfredo sauce is one of the oldest sauces of Rome. It uses egg yolks to cloak pasta in a rich, golden glaze. The classic mixture is little more than eggs and cheese. I've modified that mixture in this recipe with a lot of chopped fresh herbs. The exact combination of herbs is up to you. Use what is freshest and brightest but avoid using too much of the more assertive varieties, like rosemary or oregano. As with all sauces that use raw egg yolk, food toxins are a possibility. The heat of the pasta will cook the egg but not enough to kill bacteria. If you are unsure of the safety of your eggs, you might want to skip this recipe.

---

1 pound pasta, any shape

2 cloves garlic, minced

1/4 cup chopped fresh herbs (any combination of Italian parsley, basil, dill, tarragon, chives, rosemary, thyme, oregano, savory, or chervil)

2 egg yolks

1/3 cup freshly grated Parmesan or Romano cheese

Salt and freshly ground black pepper to taste

Bring a large pot of lightly salted water to a boil. Add the pasta and stir a few times to ensure that the pasta does not stick to itself. Boil vigorously for the time recommended on the pasta package or until the pasta is tender.

While the pasta cooks, mix the garlic, herbs, and egg yolks in a serving bowl. When the pasta is done, spoon 1/4 cup of the pasta cooking water into the serving bowl and mix into the yolks and herbs.

Drain the pasta and toss it in the serving bowl with the yolk mixture, cheese, salt, and pepper.

Smoked Salmon, Asparagus, and Lemon Ricotta Sauce

**Makes
4 servings**

This is a most beautiful and sophisticated sauce. The pink of the salmon and the vivid green asparagus spears make for an elegant contrast. The lightly salted fish also acts as a seasoning, blending naturally with the fresh dill and lemon.

1 pound curly pasta, such as rotelle

12 medium asparagus spears, trimmed and cut in 2-inch lengths

1 cup ricotta cheese

Finely grated zest and juice of 1 medium lemon

1 tablespoon walnut or extra-virgin olive oil

Salt and freshly ground black pepper to taste

4 ounces sliced smoked Nova Scotia salmon, cut in strips

2 tablespoons finely chopped fresh dill

¹/₄ cup finely chopped walnuts

Bring a large pot of lightly salted water to a boil. Add the pasta and stir a few times to ensure that the pasta does not stick to itself. Boil vigorously for the time recommended on the pasta package or until the pasta is tender. Three minutes before the pasta will finish cooking, add the asparagus pieces to the pot.

While the pasta cooks, mix the ricotta, lemon zest, lemon juice, oil, salt, and pepper in a serving bowl. Drain the pasta and asparagus and toss them with the cheese mixture in the bowl. Mix in the smoked salmon, dill, and walnuts.

Sun-Dried Tomato Paste

**Makes
4 servings**

Sun-dried tomatoes are little flavor factories, pumping out the taste of tomato far beyond their puny proportions. Use tomatoes packed in oil. If you have only plain dried tomatoes, you must first rehydrate them with boiling water and cure them in oil overnight before cooking with them.

1 pound pasta, any shape
12 sun-dried tomatoes packed in olive oil
Pinch of crushed red pepper flakes
2 cloves garlic

¹/₄ cup oil from sun-dried tomatoes or
  ¹/₄ cup extra-virgin olive oil
Salt and freshly ground black pepper to taste
¹/₃ cup freshly grated Parmesan cheese

Bring a large pot of lightly salted water to a boil. Add the pasta and stir a few times to ensure that the pasta does not stick to itself. Boil vigorously for the time recommended on the pasta package or until the pasta is tender.

While the pasta cooks, purée the sun-dried tomatoes, red pepper flakes, garlic, oil, salt, and pepper in a food processor or blender.

Drain the pasta and toss it in a serving bowl with the sun-dried tomato mixture and the cheese.

Chapter 10

Creamy Sauces

Sun-Dried Tomato, Hot Pepper, and Cream Sauce

Sour Creamy Primavera Sauce

Creamy Herby Spinach Sauce

Creamy Cheddar Sauce

Wild Mushroom, Brandy, and Cream Sauce

Cream and Butter Sauce

Lemon, Garlic, and Caper Butter Sauce

Gorgonzola, Walnut, and Cream Sauce

Clam and White Bean Paste

Creamy Vidalia Sauce

Creaminess doesn't have to come from cream, but it *does* need real ingredients. Forget such nonfat cream substitutes as nonfat cheeses, sour cream, and yogurt. On the label, they may look like the new messiahs, but in real life, tested by real taste buds, they all either break at the first whisper of heat or are struck down by the awesome, flavor-dissipating properties of a plate of pasta.

What *does* work is soft, starchy vegetables, such as beans, peas, and potatoes; reduced-fat or regular sour cream; and soft cheeses, such as ricotta, chèvre, and cream cheese. The vegetables must be cooked before going into the sauce, but this can usually be done right in the pasta water, with the pasta. Sour cream and cheeses need no cooking, of course. Just remove them from the refrigerator about an hour before you use them and toss them with the pasta while it's piping hot.

But that is not what this final chapter is about. The first nine feature lots of creamy-tasting, naturally low-fat sauces. I've saved the unapologetically indulgent, I'll-eat-fat-and-be-damned recipes for the swan song.

Cream is a miraculous substance. Although its image has suffered in recent years from the general condemnation directed at any ingredient with a fat content, the fact is that cream is lower in fat than cheese or butter; it lends its silken sheen, lush texture, and natural sweetness to a sauce with no need to so much as turn on the stove; and it doesn't take very much to do the job.

Cream, like all dairy products, is an emulsion of water, butterfat, and protein. As it heats, the water evaporates, helping the cream to thicken into a sauce, but reduction is only part of the magic. More important is the protein, which gently coagulates as it heats, setting up the cream subtly without much loss in volume.

Mild acids, such as tomato or wine, encourage coagulation. This can be used to your advantage—or it can turn against you if you're not careful. When adding cream to a tomato or wine reduction, watch the heat. I usually add the cream to a hot reduction off the burner, stir it well, and see what happens before I give it any more heat. Another second or two over a medium-low flame is usually all it takes.

By contrast, cream sauces that are thickened solely by reduction tend to be pasty and overly rich. Think about it: as the amount of water in a cream sauce reduces, its percentage of fat skyrockets, turning a liquid that was 22 percent fat into one that's 60 percent fat or more.

Sun-Dried Tomato, Hot Pepper, and Cream Sauce

**Makes
4 servings**

The trick to this sauce is minimal cooking. Simmer it too long and the tomatoes will turn bitter and the cream will congeal. You can chop the tomatoes and garlic in the first minutes the pasta cooks, then heat the sauce just before the pasta is done.

1 pound pasta, any shape
1 tablespoon extra-virgin olive oil
2 cloves garlic, minced
Pinch of crushed red pepper flakes

20 sun-dried tomatoes packed in olive oil, cut
  in thin strips
$^3/_4$ cup light cream
Salt and freshly ground black pepper to taste

Bring a large pot of lightly salted water to a boil. Add the pasta and stir a few times to ensure that the pasta does not stick to itself. Boil vigorously for the time recommended on the pasta package or until the pasta is tender.

While the pasta cooks, heat the oil in a large deep skillet over medium heat, add the garlic, red pepper flakes, and sun-dried tomatoes, and stir for 10 seconds. Add the cream, salt, and pepper and bring to a boil. Remove from the heat. If the sauce thickens too much as it sits, thin it with a few tablespoons of the pasta cooking water.

Drain the pasta and toss it with the sauce in a serving bowl. Add more salt and pepper if needed.

Sour Creamy Primavera Sauce

**Makes
4 servings**

This is a very impressive, very easy sauce. Half the vegetables cook right along with the noodles, and the rest are simply sautéed. Sour cream brings it all together. Reduced-fat sour cream is fine for this preparation, but don't use fat-free varieties, which tend to separate when they're mixed with hot pasta.

---

1 pound pasta, any shape

4 ounces baby carrots, each cut in 8 strips

1/2 pound thin asparagus, trimmed and cut in 1 1/2-inch lengths

2 tablespoons olive oil

1/2 medium onion, chopped

1/4 pound mushrooms, cleaned, stemmed, and sliced

Salt and freshly ground black pepper to taste

1 red bell pepper, cut in thin strips

1/2 cup frozen peas

2/3 cup regular or reduced-fat sour cream

2 tablespoons freshly grated Parmesan or Romano cheese

Bring a large pot of lightly salted water to a boil. Add the pasta and stir a few times to ensure that the pasta does not stick to itself. Boil vigorously for the time recommended on the pasta package or until the pasta is tender. Add the carrots 5 minutes before the pasta will finish cooking, and the asparagus 1 minute before.

While the pasta cooks, heat the oil over medium-high heat in a large deep skillet, add the onion, and cook until barely softened, about 1 minute. Add the mushrooms, salt, and pepper and cook until the mushrooms lose their raw look, about 3 minutes. Add the bell pepper, cook 2 minutes, then add the peas and cook another 2 minutes.

Drain the pasta, carrots, and asparagus and toss them with the sautéed vegetables, sour cream, and cheese in a serving bowl. Add more salt and pepper if needed.

Creamy Herby Spinach Sauce

**Makes
4 servings**

*This sauce is a snap. The spinach cooks in seconds and all the flavor comes
from the herbed cream cheese that melts on contact with the hot pan. Don't
worry about ridding the cooked spinach of excess water. The small amount
of water will help loosen the cheese and give the sauce just the right creamy
fluid consistency.*

1 pound pasta, any shape

1 tablespoon olive oil

1/2 medium onion, chopped

One 10-ounce bag fresh spinach, stemmed,
washed, chopped, and left wet

6 ounces herb-and-garlic cream cheese

1/4 cup milk

Salt and freshly ground black pepper to taste

2 tablespoons freshly grated Parmesan cheese

Bring a large pot of lightly salted water to a boil. Add the pasta and stir a few
times to ensure that the pasta does not stick to itself. Boil vigorously for the
time recommended on the pasta package or until the pasta is tender.

While the pasta cooks, heat the oil over medium heat in a large deep
skillet, add the onion, and cook until softened, about 2 minutes. Add the wet
spinach, toss briefly, cover, and cook until the spinach has wilted, about 2
minutes. Mix in the cream cheese and the milk, stirring until the cheese has
melted. Season with salt and pepper.

Drain the pasta and toss it with the sauce and cheese in a serving bowl.
Add more salt and pepper if needed.

Creamy Cheddar Sauce

**Makes
4 servings**

This sauce is similar to fondue but without the built-in worry of waiting for the whole thing to disintegrate over hours of dipping. The cheese must be cut into very small pieces or shredded and tossed with cornstarch. The size helps it melt quickly without excessive heat, while the starch ensures that the sauce maintains a smooth, silken texture.

---

1 pound long pasta, such as fettuccine or spaghetti

6 ounces sharp Cheddar cheese, finely chopped or shredded

1 tablespoon cornstarch

2 tablespoons olive oil

1/2 medium onion, finely chopped

2 cloves garlic, minced

1 tablespoon green peppercorns packed in brine, drained

1 1/2 cups dry white wine

Salt and freshly ground black pepper to taste

Bring a large pot of lightly salted water to a boil. Add the pasta and stir a few times to ensure that the pasta does not stick to itself. Boil vigorously for the time recommended on the pasta package or until the pasta is tender.

While the pasta cooks, toss the cheese with the cornstarch and set aside.

Heat the oil in a medium skillet over medium-high heat, add the onion, and cook until softened, about 2 minutes. Add the garlic and green peppercorns and stir. Add the wine and boil vigorously for 1 minute. Season with salt and pepper. Just before the pasta is ready, bring the sauce back to a boil, remove it from the heat, and whisk in the cheese until the sauce is smooth.

Drain the pasta and toss it with the sauce in a serving bowl. Add more salt and pepper if needed.

Wild Mushroom, Brandy, and Cream Sauce

**Makes
4 servings**

The combination of forest mushrooms, quality brandy, and rich cream is a model of opulence. Use this recipe to various effects by altering the mushrooms. Morels give a dark, earthy flavor; chanterelles are less intense and brighter; and oyster mushrooms or shiitakes make a more casual and subtle flavor. I have found one of the assortments of wild mushrooms available at most markets to be most convenient and delicious in this recipe.

---

1 pound pasta, any shape

2 tablespoons olive oil

½ medium onion, chopped

½ pound fresh wild mushroom caps
   (any type), cleaned and sliced

Salt and freshly ground black pepper to taste

2 cloves garlic, minced

1 teaspoon soy sauce

¼ cup brandy

⅔ cup light cream

1 tablespoon freshly grated Parmesan cheese

Bring a large pot of lightly salted water to a boil. Add the pasta and stir a few times to ensure that the pasta does not stick to itself. Boil vigorously for the time recommended on the pasta package or until the pasta is tender.

While the pasta cooks, heat the oil in a large deep skillet over medium-high heat. Add the onion and cook until barely softened, about 1 minute. Add the mushrooms, salt, and pepper and cook until the mushrooms lose their raw look, about 3 minutes. Add the garlic, soy sauce, and brandy and bring to a boil. Add the cream and return to a boil. Adjust the salt and pepper and boil for 1 minute.

Drain the pasta and toss it with the sauce and cheese in a serving bowl. Add more salt and pepper if needed.

Cream and Butter Sauce

**Makes
4 servings**

I don't care that the Center for Science in the Public Interest has deemed Fettuccine Alfredo synonymous with cardinal sin and certain death. The sauce remains one of the most delicious pasta embellishments ever devised, even with the slightly reduced amount of cream and butter that this version calls for. As long as you don't become an Alfredo junkie, I believe that an occasional indulgence is worth the threatened risk. I like to think of it as mental-health food. Besides, it's a snap. The only cooking, other than boiling the pasta, is melting the butter.

---

1 pound pasta, any shape
2 tablespoons butter
1/2 cup heavy cream

Grating of fresh nutmeg
5 tablespoons freshly grated Parmesan cheese
Salt and freshly ground black pepper to taste

Bring a large pot of lightly salted water to a boil. Add the pasta and stir a few times to ensure that the pasta does not stick to itself. Boil vigorously for the time recommended on the pasta package or until the pasta is tender.

While the pasta cooks, melt the butter in a large deep skillet over medium heat.

Drain the pasta and toss it in a serving bowl with the melted butter, cream, nutmeg, cheese, salt, and pepper.

Lemon, Garlic, and Caper Butter Sauce

**Makes
4 servings**

*This flavored butter is brightened by lemon juice, bits of lemon zest, and sparks
of salty capers. Once the butter has melted, the sauce takes only a few seconds
more to prepare.*

---

1 pound pasta, any shape

1 medium lemon

2 tablespoons olive oil

4 tablespoons butter

3 tablespoons capers

3 cloves garlic, minced

Salt and freshly ground black pepper to taste

2 tablespoon freshly grated Romano cheese

Bring a large pot of lightly salted water to a boil. Add the pasta and stir a few
times to ensure that the pasta does not stick to itself. Boil vigorously for the
time recommended on the pasta package or until the pasta is tender.

While the pasta cooks, remove the lemon zest with a zester or fine-tooth
grater, then squeeze the lemon juice. Set aside the zest and juice separately.

Heat the oil in a large deep skillet over medium heat, then add and melt
half the butter. Add the capers, lemon zest, lemon juice, and garlic and cook for
1 minute. Remove from the heat. Mix in the remaining butter and add the salt
and pepper.

Drain the pasta and toss it with the sauce and cheese in a serving bowl.
Add more salt and pepper if needed.

Gorgonzola, Walnut, and Cream Sauce

**Makes
4 servings**

Gorgonzola, the mild, sweet blue cheese from the mountains of northern Italy, is almost a sauce in and of itself. It melts effortlessly into a smooth cream. In this recipe, crisply toasted walnuts are a counterpoint to its creaminess.

---

1 pound shaped pasta, such as shells or raddiatore

1 tablespoon olive oil

$^2/_3$ cup walnut pieces, chopped

2 cloves garlic, minced

Salt and freshly ground black pepper to taste

Pinch of cayenne pepper

4 ounces Gorgonzola cheese, crumbled

$^1/_3$ cup heavy cream

Bring a large pot of lightly salted water to a boil. Add the pasta and stir a few times to ensure that the pasta does not stick to itself. Boil vigorously for the time recommended on the pasta package or until the pasta is tender.

While the pasta cooks, heat the oil in a large deep skillet over medium-high heat, add the walnuts, and cook, stirring constantly, until toasted, about 2 minutes. Remove from the heat, add the garlic, and season with salt, pepper, and cayenne.

Drain the pasta and toss it in a serving bowl with the walnuts, Gorgonzola, and cream, adding more salt and pepper if needed.

Clam and White Bean Paste

**Makes
4 servings**

The "cream" in this sauce is fat-free. Rather than coming from the dairy, it begins life as cannellini beans that are mashed before they melt into a creamy coating for the pasta. In the coastal cuisines of northern Italy, white beans are traditionally paired with seafood and clams to make one of the best matches. If you can't find cannellini (white kidney beans), a smaller variety, such as Great Northern or pea beans, will work fine.

2 dozen littleneck clams

1 pound shaped pasta, such as large shells
  or raddiatore

1/4 cup extra-virgin olive oil

1 medium onion, chopped

2 cloves garlic, minced

1 cup dry white wine

1/4 cup chopped fresh dill

1 cup cooked cannellini beans, homemade
  or canned, drained

Salt and freshly ground black pepper to taste

Place the clams in a large bowl, cover with cold water, swirl in the water to remove surface dirt, drain, and cover again with fresh water.

Bring a large pot of lightly salted water to a boil. Add the pasta and stir a few times to ensure that the pasta does not stick to itself. Boil vigorously for the time recommended on the pasta package or until the pasta is tender.

While the pasta cooks, heat the olive oil in a large deep skillet over medium-high heat, add the onion, and cook until softened, about 2 minutes. Add the garlic and wine and bring to a boil. Drain the clams and add them to the skillet. Add the dill, cover the pan, and cook until the clams open, about 4 minutes. Add the beans and return the mixture to a boil. Use the back of a large fork or spoon to mash about one-quarter of the beans. Season with salt and pepper.

Drain the pasta and toss it with the sauce in a serving bowl.

Creamy Vidalia Sauce

**Makes
4 servings**

The trick to this flavorful sauce is selecting a sugar-packed onion and cooking it to encourage its sweetness to emerge. By starting the onions in a dry skillet, their moisture is drawn out along with all the water-soluble sugars. Once the juices are released, butter and oil are added, triggering development of a more pungent onion flavor. Sour cream finishes the sauce, providing a lush vehicle for the complex onion flavors.

---

1 pound long pasta, such as fettuccine or spaghetti

3 large Vidalia (or other sweet) onions, halved and thinly sliced

2 tablespoons butter

2 tablespoons olive oil

2 cloves garlic, minced

1/2 cup sour cream, regular or reduced-fat

1/4 cup freshly grated Parmesan cheese

Salt and white pepper to taste

Bring a large pot of lightly salted water to a boil. Add the pasta and stir a few times to ensure that the pasta does not stick to itself. Boil vigorously for the time recommended on the pasta package or until the pasta is tender.

While the pasta cooks, place the onions in a large nonstick skillet, cover, and cook over medium heat until the onions are soft and moist, about 5 minutes. Uncover, increase the heat to high, add the butter and the oil, and cook for 5 more minutes, stirring frequently, until the onions are a pale golden brown. Stir in the garlic. Remove from the heat, stir in the sour cream and cheese, and season with salt and pepper.

Drain the pasta and toss it with the sauce in a serving bowl.

Index

A

Aïoli
    anchovy, 104
    rosemary and sage, 19
Alfredo sauce, herbed, 110
Almond pesto, smoky, 18
Anchovy
    aïoli, 104
    and roasted pepper sauce, 30
    Romano, and garlic sauce, 80
Artichoke
    marinated, and feta sauce, 33
    tomato, and feta sauce, 107
Arugula, prosciutto, and aged
    ricotta sauce, 109
Asiago cheese, xvii, 77, 78
Asparagus
    shrimp, and dill sauce, 56
    smoked salmon, and lemon
      ricotta sauce, 111

B

Basil
    -chicken sauce thickened with white
      beans, 50
    lemon pesto, 17
    mussels rosa, 55
    and prosciutto sauce, 16
    smoky almond pesto, 18
    tomato, and chèvre sauce, 35
    tomato, and cream, 8
    tomato salsa, 103
Bean(s)
    green, lemon garlic sauce, 67
    red, chili tomato sauce with, 4
    white, and clam paste, 123
    white, chicken-basil sauce thickened
      with, 50
Beef
    everyday meat sauce, 41
    mushroom sauce, stir-fried, 92

C

P

Parmesan cheese, xvi–xvii, 77, 78
  broccoli, and garlic sauce, 65
  carbonara sauce, 81
  four-cheese sauce stunned with
    garlic, 87
  herbed Alfredo sauce, 110
  mushroom, and tomato sauce, 86
  Parmigiano Reggiano, xvi, 78
  winter squash, and pine nuts
    sauce, 66
Parsley, xx–xxi
  garlic, and cheese sauce, 15
  spicy herbed mushroom
    sauce, 24
Pasta, xiii–xv
  water for cooking, xv–xvi, xxiii
Peas
  baby, tomato and cream sauce, 72
  and prosciutto sauce, 38
Pecorino Romano cheese, xvii
Pepper, bell
  olive salsa, 108
  three-pepper sauce, 74
Pepper, black, watercress, and
  chèvre sauce, 21
Pepper, chili
  chipotle tomato sauce, 10
  clam sauce, 54
  and pumpkin seed pesto, 36
  three-pepper sauce, 74

Pepper(s), roasted, xix
  and anchovy sauce, 30
  and ricotta sauce, 79
  three-pepper sauce, 74
  tomato sauce, 6
Pesto, 14
  lemon basil, 17
  smoky almond, 18
Pine nuts, winter squash, and
  cheese sauce, 66
Pork
  and cilantro sauce, chilied, 45
  and shrimp sauce, stir-fried, 98
Potato(es), xix
  and broccoli rabe sauce with
    lotsa garlic, 69
  and dill sauce, 25
  stir-fried savory turkey
    sauce, 96
Poultry
  chicken and olive sauce, 44
  chicken-basil sauce thickened
    with white beans, 50
  chicken livers in sour cream sauce, 48
  everyday meat sauce, 41
  stir-fried herb chicken
    sauce, 99
  stir-fried kraut and chicken liver
    sauce, 97
  stir-fried savory turkey
    sauce, 96
  turkey Bolognese sauce, 42

Primavera sauce
    sour creamy, 116
    stir-fried, 91
Prosciutto
    arugula, and aged ricotta
        sauce, 109
    and basil sauce, 16
    and peas sauce, 38
Provolone cheese, xxiii
    four-cheese sauce stunned with
        garlic, 87
Pumpkin seed and chili pesto, 36

R

Ricotta cheese
    and roasted red pepper sauce, 79
    sauce, smoked salmon, asparagus,
        and lemon, 111
Ricotta salata
    arugula, and prosciutto sauce, 109
    four-cheese sauce stunned with
        garlic, 87
Romano cheese, xvii, 77, 78
    anchovy, and garlic sauce, 80
    broccoli, and garlic sauce, 65
    four-cheese sauce stunned
        with garlic, 87
    herbed Alfredo sauce, 110
    parsley, and garlic sauce, 15
    Pecorino spinach sauce, 73
    winter squash, and pine nuts
        sauce, 66

Roquefort cheese
    spinach, and garlic sauce, 105
    walnut, and fennel sauce, 34
Rosemary
    and corn sauce, smoky, 31
    and sage aïoli, 19
    salmon, and capers sauce, 57

S

Saffron, fennel, and shrimp
    sauce, 20
Sage and rosemary aïoli, 19
Salmon
    capers, and rosemary sauce, 57
    smoked, asparagus, and lemon
        ricotta sauce, 111
Salsa
    olive pepper, 108
    tomato basil, 103
Sardine and olive sauce, 61
Sauce texture, adjusting, xxiii
Sausage
    and mushroom sauce, 43
    in white clam sauce, 46
Scallop(s), xx
    lemon sauce, 62
Seafood sauces, 51–62
    crab, herb cheese, and
        spinach, 59
    crab, tarragon, and cream, 53
    hot pepper clam, 54
    lemon scallop, 62

W